M000222063

OPEN
YOUR
OWN
DOORS

To Nopalie —
Thank you for always
believing in me!

Nora Castro   10.11.21

OPEN YOUR OWN DOORS

ONE WOMAN'S STORY OF SUCCESS IN A MALE-DOMINATED INDUSTRY

NORA CASTRO

THIRD KING

Published by Third King, Johnson City, Texas
www.noracastro.com

Edited and designed by Girl Friday Productions
www.girlfridayproductions.com

Cover design: Rachel Marek
Project management: Devon Fredericksen
Editorial management: Laura Dailey

ISBN (hardcover): 978-1-7372926-2-3
ISBN (paperback): 978-1-7372926-0-9
ISBN (ebook): 978-1-7372926-1-6

Library of Congress Control Number: 2021912747

To my husband, Robby. For the past twenty years, he has given me his insights, his guidance, and his unwavering support. He provided me with a road map as I blazed my own trail. Without him, I would not be where I am today.

And to my uncle, Don Howarth, who provided a beacon of what I could be.

CONTENTS

PREFACE. xi

CHAPTER ONE: HOW IT ALL BEGAN FOR ME 1
Starting Out in the Financial Services Industry. . . 3
The Importance of Personal Planning 5
Career Objectives and Educational Decisions . . . 6
Personal Relationships and Family. 7
Fun and Recreation 8
Financial Planning. 9
Finding My Own Voice 11

CHAPTER TWO: CONTROL YOUR OWN LIFE 17
Visualize What You Want. 18
Watch Out for Deal-Breakers 20
Manage Your Curveballs. 22
Seize Control. 24

CHAPTER THREE: ACCEPT BOTH NATURE AND NURTURE. 29
Embrace the Duality 30
Know Your Options 33
Turn Dreams into Goals. 34
Have a Flexible Plan B 38

CHAPTER FOUR: GET TO KNOW—AND BE COMFORTABLE WITH—YOURSELF . . 41
Create Space for Yourself. 42
Get Organized. 43

CONTENTS

Evaluate Your Work/Life Balance 45
Celebrate Yourself 46
Anticipate the Crossroads 48
Identify Your Destination 51
Leave It at the Office 54
Design Your Own Environment 55
Learn to Be Yourself 59
Do the Opposite 62
Accept Your Failures 65

CHAPTER FIVE: LOVE WHAT YOU DO 67
Find and Follow Your Passion 68
Love Your Career 70
Stay Focused on Your Passion 72

CHAPTER SIX: SURVIVE AND FLOURISH 75
Avoid Sexual Misunderstandings and Advances . . 76
Learn to Read the Room 77
Learn to Delegate 80
Know Your Strengths 80
Get Yourself Promoted 82
Become Unstoppable 83

CHAPTER SEVEN: MANAGE YOUR CLIENTS AND YOUR TEAM 85
Manage with Integrity 86
Communicate Effectively 87
Train and Support Your Team 90
Respond with Common Courtesy 98
Develop Realistic Expectations 99
Manage Inevitable Problems 100

CONTENTS

CHAPTER EIGHT: AVOID REGRETS AND FACE YOUR FEARS 102

Let Go 103

Look to the Future, Love Who You Are,

and Avoid Jealousy 104

Face Your Fears 107

Choose Your Tomorrow. 108

CHAPTER NINE: GIVE BACK. 111

Open Horizons for Others 112

Control Where Your Money Goes. 117

CHAPTER TEN: PLAN FOR RETIREMENT—NOW 121

Plan Your Money 122

Plan Your Time 124

Watch for Detours and Obstacles. 127

Use Caution with Sudden Wealth 129

Take It Slowly 130

CHAPTER ELEVEN: A LOOK INTO MY LIFE 132

Getting the Day Started 133

Listening to My Needs. 135

Setting Goals. 137

ACKNOWLEDGMENTS 141

ABOUT THE AUTHOR 143

NOTES. 145

PREFACE

Someone came forward to help me: someone who had faith in my abilities; someone who saw potential in me where others might not, someone who risked their own reputation to advance my career. I have never forgotten those people and I know that anything I achieved in my life was a result of others who have helped me along the way.

—US Navy Admiral William H. McRaven (retired), *Make Your Bed*

When I first read those words, I thought, *Wow! How different from my own journey, but how wonderful it would have been to have had people helping me along the way. It could have saved me from paying some heavy dues. McRaven's experience must be the very definition of* male privilege.

After reading Charles Darwin's *On the Origin of Species*, Herbert Spencer coined the phrase "survival of the fittest." In today's male-dominated business world, it is not just that a woman needs to learn to succeed with little or no help from others; it's also the "survival of she who can adapt." In the following pages, you will read how one woman succeeded with little help from others and adapted, time after time, to achieve her goals.

I would like to imagine that this book could become required reading for all male managers. They would get better at their jobs if they knew what their staff, including the women, were feeling and dealing with daily. But my primary purpose is to let *women* readers know this: you are not alone. I hope the lessons I've learned, and am passing on here, will provide knowledge and tools to help you not just survive, but thrive, by giving you the confidence to adapt, achieve, and stand up for yourself.

I am proud to report that this book is already a success. A friend of mine was about to apply for a major executive job with a large corporation when I asked her to review a first draft of my manuscript. The job would be a major step up for her. After reading what I had written, she told me she knew she had the experience, qualifications, and personality to do the job. And then she told me: "What concerned me most was asking for the compensation package that I knew the job deserved and that any man would demand. After reading your book, I set my concerns aside, walked in with a positive attitude, and didn't hesitate to tell them the compensation package it would take to hire me. Nora, I start Monday. What great advice. Thank you!"

Hopefully reading this book will result in similar positive experiences for you as you learn to *let nothing stand in your way*.

CHAPTER ONE

HOW IT ALL BEGAN FOR ME

If you know the enemy and know yourself, you need not fear the result of a hundred battles. If you know yourself but not the enemy, for every victory gained you will also suffer a defeat. If you know neither the enemy nor yourself, you will succumb in every battle.

—Sun Tzu, *The Art of War*

When reading a book, I like to know an author's credentials right up front. If an author's name is followed by a lot of three-letter academic degrees and the book is based primarily on research and studies, I don't waste my money. I prefer books based on real-life experiences. Similarly, my book is based solely on one woman's story of real-life experiences surviving and thriving in a male-dominated industry. What do I mean by male-dominated? Look at it this way: throughout my forty-year career, not one of my managers was a woman. Does that sound familiar? Even if you have not yet experienced a job where you are surrounded by men, you probably will at some point in your life. So let me prepare you and provide you with the tools to cope.

I do have academic credentials: I earned a bachelor of science degree in business administration from the University of Southern California. But as you will soon read, these credentials have little to do with the career I have pursued. I did not realize until I became a working woman that business is not about lessons learned in the classroom; it's about the application of common sense and practice.

As a matter of fact, my initial college plans had nothing to do with business. I had intended to follow in my older brother Ivan's footsteps and become a doctor—specifically, a forensic pathologist. As happens to many people, though, a chance encounter—while I was looking for a work-study job to finance my education—changed my life. I met a stockbroker, and he offered me a job. At about the same time, I had another one of those life-changing experiences that confirmed I was on the right path. I had been dating a guy whose family had a home on Little Balboa Island, south of Los Angeles, and he took me sailing. While on his boat, I witnessed an amazing view of dolphins jumping and frolicking right alongside our vessel. It was at that moment I realized I could not spend my life inside a laboratory. I knew I had to be out in the world, frolicking and experiencing life. And I had already learned that I enjoyed studying supply-and-demand graphs more than chemistry. So I changed my major from pre-med to economics.

Starting Out in the Financial Services Industry

Now my world felt right. At the young age of eighteen, I accepted that stockbroker's offer for a position at his Beverly Hills financial firm. I was now employed by one of the leading investment banks in America.

I started as a receptionist, and within a few months I was promoted to sales assistant. After that, through hard work and an intuitive understanding of the business, I quickly worked my way up the ladder to become a registered representative—by the age of twenty.

As an entry-level portfolio manager, I knew I was still far from having my own office in the executive suite, and I knew I had a lot to learn about the investment business. I also had a lot to learn about taking care of my own finances. One of the things I learned early on was that owning a house, as quickly as possible, was a wise investment. And working at the Beverly Hills firm allowed me to do that. I bought my first house at the age of twenty-three. But all this success did not come easily. Being on the West Coast, where the time is three hours earlier than on Wall Street, I worked from six in the morning until three in the afternoon and then drove to USC and took classes from four until ten. I ultimately graduated in 1988, and although I left the Beverly Hills firm in 1989 when it went bankrupt, I had discovered my love for the demanding and exciting investment industry—an industry I have never left. I also learned a critical lesson about my chosen field: changing firms was not only common; it was almost a requirement in order to move up.

Recognizing that, I moved up the ladder from firm to firm, finally becoming senior vice president and investment officer at a firm where I worked for eight years, starting my own investment firm within that company. But I was blown out of the water when the tech bubble burst in 1999. Fortunately, by then I had developed good client relations and team management skills. In Chapter 7 I will show you how to do the same. These skills enabled me to survive the fallout by preserving my client base and my team. With the impending bankruptcy in 2008 of the firm where I'd worked for eight years, I moved to a different firm as a senior vice president, bringing most of my clients with me. There, I focused on portfolio strategy, financial planning, and estate preservation strategies. I was one of a small handful of women at each of these firms who had learned how to survive in this highly competitive, male-dominated industry.

In 2019 I joyfully made what I hope will be my last move, when I transitioned my practice to a nationally renowned financial firm. Here I am able to focus on holistic financial planning with a group of clients I genuinely love. I was recently named to the *Forbes* America's Top Women Wealth Advisors list for the fourth straight year, every year since the inauguration of the award in 2018. Can you believe there wasn't such an award until then? This is truly an honor, since the *Forbes* ranking was developed by SHOOK Research and is based on an algorithm of quantitative data, such as revenue trends and assets under management, as well as qualitative data, including telephone and in-person interviews, a review of best practices, service and investing models, and compliance records. For those who might find it interesting, I was also the feature of a *Forbes* magazine article, which was published last year and can be found at Forbes.com.

While financial planning is what I've devoted my career to, it's not the focus of this book. My aim in these pages is to show how some fundamental principles and guidelines that I've learned throughout my career can help you design and navigate your own career—and life—path. Let's look at a few that I will go into in more detail in later chapters.

The Importance of Personal Planning

One thing is assured: life goes by fast. Do not face it without plans for now, for the remainder of your working life, and for the twenty- or thirty-something years you will be retired. As will be explained in more detail in Chapter 3, dreams can become goals with a plan. Many, if not most, people let their education, their career, and their entire life just happen. Don't let that be you. If you start planning and taking charge of your life because of what you read in this book, you will have made one of my *own* dreams come true.

Career Objectives and Educational Decisions

One of the first major decisions most young people make is what type of education to pursue. This might mean an undergraduate degree, a master's, or even a PhD. It may be vocational training. It may mean learning another language in order to get the international job you have always wanted. As you have just read, my own career direction was more due to being in the right place at the right time, more coincidental than planned. And I will venture that was the case for many of you. My brother Ivan knew exactly what he wanted to do and was passionate about it, and that is what he did. I'm sure, as a high schooler, that my decision to become a forensic pathologist was primarily the result of a younger sister looking up to her older brother, whom she admired. I had watched the television series *Quincy, M.E.* growing up and was madly interested in the field. I had thought it would be a career about which I was truly passionate. However, my real passion came when I was exposed to the financial services industry.

My experience has been that many young people are like I was. They may have some idea about a future career, but as they get out into the world, their horizons expand, opportunities present themselves, and they end up going in a very different direction. For those of you not yet in a chosen profession that you love, and whether or not you have already attended college, my advice is to work for a year or two in or around a profession you think you may want to pursue before deciding what, if any, additional education you might require. If you have not yet paid for a college education, that could save you an untold amount of time and money on educational expenses that have no relevancy to your ultimate career.

The best advice I have ever heard regarding career and education, which I will go into in more detail in Chapter 5, was related to me by a friend as advice he gave his children. "If you have a passion, pursue it with all of your energy. If you do that, however much money you make, or don't make, will be enough."

Personal Relationships and Family

Both of these demand time and money. Don't let personal relationships just happen; be proactive and plan. Do you want to have a close, personal, one-on-one relationship? Do you want to have children? If those are your goals, how are you going to accomplish them? Know that neither of those is a requirement for a happy, fulfilling life. Don't worry; if those *are* your goals, I have advice later on how to accomplish them. In Chapter 2 I will tell you how I made the conscious decision to not have children of my own and why it has been the right decision for me.

Fun and Recreation

We all need to have fun! If you want to excel at a sport or take up a new hobby in the future, plan it now. When I graduated from USC, a girlfriend and I decided we wanted to take up skiing. We did not have much money, so we planned carefully. We would drive to a mountain late Friday night after we got off work, sleep in the parking lot at the foot of the hill, and get up when the lifts first opened. It was great, and we spent the next several years skiing almost all of the western states.

I had another friend who, like me, loved to travel. We were both young and adventurous, but since finances were tight, we planned our trips based on places in the world that had just had a nearby crisis. For example, when there was a crisis in Jakarta and most tourists had canceled their travel plans, we hopped on a plane to nearby Bali to snorkel at reduced rates and with very few tourists. And when the wall was coming down in Germany and everyone wanted to go to Berlin, we flew to nearby France and had a memorable experience in Paris. With careful, creative planning, we were able to accomplish so much at relatively little expense.

Of course, we had youth and energy on our side, and the younger you start your planning, the better. But you are never too old to start, which brings me to the next topic, financial planning, which is, of course, my chosen profession, and one I started at a young age. It's also an industry entirely dominated by men and one in which I paid some heavy dues to learn the lessons I am passing on to you. Hopefully my story and words of advice will smooth your path to success.

Financial Planning

Before taking the job at the Beverly Hills firm, I had never thought about financial planning. Does anyone when they are that young? I cannot stress enough how fortunate I was to learn its importance so early in life. Let me say this as bluntly as I can—financial planning needs to be an important focus for you and your family, regardless of your age, the career you are pursuing, or the stage of your current career. It is especially important for young women. Why? Because, unless you inherit it, there are only three ways for a woman to make money:

1. Work hard, save your earnings, and invest them smartly.
2. Marry wealth, which could potentially require as much work as any other job.

3. Win the lottery, which probably has about the same odds as marrying wealth.

It is important that you learn about and take charge of your personal finances, no matter where your money comes from. You need to live on a budget. Create expense worksheets to see where your money is going. Write down your dreams and figure out a plan to achieve them. You say you don't have the time? It will require less time than planning a Disney World trip with your children or a glamping weekend with your girlfriends. The point is, plan and save. Save and plan. You might think you are too young right now to think about those later years, but I speak from experience—my own and that of my clients: retirement comes fast! How many people in their sixties and seventies have been hired at your workplace? We will explore this more in Chapter 10, but it's never too soon to start thinking about saving for the future.

Today, my practice is focused predominantly on women, especially those who are recently widowed or are going through a divorce. I have made this a focus because I understand how harrowing those transitions in life can be, both emotionally and financially. It is at these times that my clients want and need me to be right at their side to help them navigate choppy waters. The first task is invariably to help them find the money and assets, which, without someone like me who has done it many times, is not an easy task. Then comes the part I enjoy so much: working with them to plan their lives going ahead in accordance with their goals, whether that is to take care of parents and children or to otherwise find and enjoy the things they most want from life.

Finding My Own Voice

It might sound as if my journey to this point has been relatively easy, but quite the opposite is true. I have struggled and cried in desperation as I've made my way through this male-dominated industry over the years. I have often felt I'm in a dream, that one where you scream, and no one hears. That feeling of being invisible is particularly evident as I think back to a conference I once attended. It was designed for potential future managers, and I was so happy and proud to have been chosen as a management candidate, especially because there had yet to be any female managers in the division of the company where I worked. When the conference leader asked if anyone was ready to become a manager, I enthusiastically raised my hand. At this point in my career, I was single, willing to relocate anywhere, and ready to make my mark in the executive suite. But later in the day, my enthusiasm was shattered when four of my colleagues, all men, were chosen to select teams for an activity. It was like a game at the school-yard, and to my dismay, I was the last one picked. I went into the women's restroom, cried and yelled, and returned to the conference disheartened and defeated. Yet, I have survived. Sadly, though, I must admit that after almost four decades of trying to make life better for the women who came after me, I am afraid that I have failed. The numbers are clear: Forty years ago, the percentage of women in the financial services industry was 14 percent. Today it's only 12 percent. Hopefully, this book will help change that by encouraging more women to pursue careers in my industry and by making the male managers and executives who might read what I have written more aware of how to work with their women colleagues and how valuable we can be in expanding and strengthening the industry.

Survival has not been without a cost to my mental well-being. After decades of fighting for office space and grasping for attention to the problems of women in my industry, I've changed. I've become what all women who survive my industry become: an exacting taskmaster. I'm also like a porcupine who is constantly on the offense. When anyone comes too close, and I perceive them to be a threat, I might hurt their feelings. I might make them feel small and pedestrian. I try to get them before they get me. I look for weak spots, and I keep dossiers on everyone. I have come to trust no one until I know their motivations and have checked their data. More than once I've had male colleagues come and tell me, "I've got this great young female assistant working for me who I think would be more comfortable working for you." When I check further, I often discover that the young assistant does not show up on time or does not do what she is asked. And she is not liked by anyone in the office. Thanks, but *no thanks*. Deal with your own hiring mistake.

I also don't let myself be swayed by emotions, and I don't automatically see the good in everyone. In any conversation with a manager, I start from the premise that they do not have my best interests at heart. I never let my guard down. While, as a woman, I must be tough and always on guard, the most important thing I must do to flourish in my industry is to be more successful than my male counterparts. Even in my own office, it's the only way my voice can be heard over the din of whoops and back-slapping congratulations given to men for their achievements, which are often much lesser than my own.

As a top-ten performer at one of my previous firms, I was invited to New York City to join a small group of top-performing men to meet with the president of my division. I stayed near Times Square and was feeling rather good about myself. At the meeting, the president bemoaned how the industry was dying and then gave us a challenge: "If you have the answer for how to save our industry, I will put up a statue in your honor in front of the corporate headquarters." I immediately raised my hand. When no one acknowledged me, I said in a loud voice, "I have the answer! I have the answer! I know how to save our industry." When there was no response, I added, "What percentage of the executives in our firm are women?"

Silence.

"What percentage are minorities?" I asked.

More silence.

Still speaking loudly, I asked, "Don't you think a Chinese client would like to deal with a Chinese advisor? Don't you think women would like to deal with other women?"

Still more silence. It was as if I didn't exist.

I then gave them the answer: "The way to save our industry is to hire and promote more women and minorities."

Giving no response, the president turned and walked out of the room. The meeting was over. All the men started getting up and talking among themselves. I was left standing alone—and I never did get my statue.

Speaking up is critical, and an important lesson I've learned is not to be dissuaded when no one seems to be listening. Rather, as Sun Tzu advised, "You must know yourself but know your enemy better." For close to forty years, I've learned that my number one enemy, in the financial services industry, has been men. They are my enemy when they will not even listen to or consider my ideas. They are my enemy when they will not grant me the same resources and rewards that were granted to men in similar situations. And they are my enemy when they will not accept me as a colleague. Can you believe I've never been asked to dinner at a male counterpart's home? I assume the men are worried about what their wives might think. And until I joined my current firm, I had never even been asked to lunch by a manager. I have few industry friends, partly because the turnover rate is remarkably high in my field, but also because, I must admit, my experience has been that the type of person who is attracted to a fast-paced, highly compensated, stressful job does not normally make a good friend. Fortunately, I have plenty of friends elsewhere, so hopefully I'm not that type of person.

I built my multimillion-dollar business with, essentially, one-fifth of an assistant while my male counterparts often had two or more. When I asked for more assistance as my practice grew, I was told to spend my own money. I was never given accounts—no male colleague retired and gave me his book of clients, for instance. I did not even receive leads for new business the way the guys did. I had to get every single client on my own, using my own wits. And of course, I was never offered a partnership. I have fought for every piece of business, every corner office, and every award.

I was often given prizes such as XL men's golf shirts, and I was once awarded a men's golf jacket with my name stitched on it: *Mr. Noro Castro*. On another occasion, I was at an event where we were split into teams, and the losing team members had to serve the other team their lunches—with shirts off. And, last but not least, men showed they were my enemy when they did not *see* or hear me, like the time at that conference when my suggestion for how to save the industry was flat-out ignored. Being treated as invisible may have been the harshest form of discrimination of all.

I will acknowledge that I'm in a cutthroat industry, but just imagine how much more difficult it has been when most decisions are made by, and from the viewpoint of, a white male. How could that possibly have fit my needs or helped me? Fortunately, I grew up with brothers. I learned to take the hits and to outlast, outthink, and outrun the boys. This has served me well.

As you can imagine, few men in my industry like me. I'm considered a threat and rightfully so. How have I dealt with this? I learned to turn this situation to my advantage. My hope for readers is that the lessons I've learned, and my resultant successes, will offer inspiration for how to survive and thrive in any male-dominated industry, and even how to deal with male supervisors and colleagues in friendlier fields. I have held little back; the trials, tribulations, and failures that have gotten me to this point are laid bare in the following chapters—along with my triumphs. Hopefully, hearing about my journey will help you on your own.

CHAPTER TWO

CONTROL YOUR OWN LIFE

There is a truth deep down inside of you that has been waiting for you to discover it, and that truth is this: you deserve all good things life has to offer.

—Rhonda Byrne, *The Secret*

Y ou can only consider yourself successful if you are happy in your own life. Ask ten people what happiness means, and you will get ten different answers. For me, happiness is finding peace with myself and the life that I've created. I have numerous clients and friends who are professionally successful but come to me reporting that they are truly unhappy with their lives. What I offer them is this exercise: train yourself to visualize the outcome you want for each day.

Visualize What You Want

In Chapter 1 I touched on planning—specifically, financial planning. Planning is so important in all aspects of life that it will come up repeatedly. For now, I want to focus on visualizing, which is part of planning—but a step beyond—and is an important part of making your plans come true. For example, my current plan includes working with clients with whom I enjoy speaking. I visualize that kind of client every time I pick up the phone. On a larger scale, I visualize what I want out of my overall career. In the beginning, my plan was to travel the world and be in management. So that is what I visualized and accomplished. But by the time I had spent twenty-seven years jet-setting around the world, I discovered how exhausting it could be. As life changed, so did my definition of happiness. To achieve a recent plan, I visualized a home on a ranch surrounded by animals so I could feel refreshed when I got to the office and happy to return home at the end of each busy day. I found that ranch life and fulfilled that vision. As I revise my plans and visualizations to achieve them, I'm not betraying my earlier yearnings; I just need to readjust from time to time to achieve what I want reality to be. Defining your own happiness is a lifelong, ever-changing exercise. But if you work hard, you can define happiness for yourself, and with a little luck mixed in, your visions will become your reality.

Visualizing your life means gaining an understanding of what you want—and what you *don't* want. When I was in my early twenties, I read a short story about a woman in Central Park who contemplated, while watching parents playing with their children and people walking their dogs, what she wanted in her own life. She asked herself, "If I look at a puppy and a baby, which would I prefer?" When I asked myself the same question, my answer was this: *I choose the puppy.* It was not that I did not like children; it was more that I considered parenting to be the hardest job in the universe, and I've always felt that I didn't have the time or skill set to be a worthy parent. However, I am an awesome aunt! I also currently have five dogs, along with a menagerie of other animals, that bring joy to my life. Am I missing one of life's greatest joys? Perhaps, but I live comfortably with my decision.

Visualizing your life, and what you want as well as what you don't want, also applies to relationships. As I mentioned, I work with a lot of widowed and divorced women, as well as those in the LGBTQ+ community. Our conversations frequently address the relationships they are in or that they have had, and sometimes the damage these relationships have left in their wake. Although I'm theoretically just their financial advisor, you would be surprised how many ask my advice about dating and finding a spouse/life partner. I tell them to approach this challenge the same way they visualize other elements of life, such as dealing with elderly parents or children, or changing jobs. Start with a plan, and then visualize a positive outcome. Let go of negative self-talk.

Watch Out for Deal-Breakers

I also advise people to watch out for the deal-breakers, which are different for everyone and will change depending upon where you are in your career and life. Dogs are an integral part of my life, so I decided I would never date someone who does not like animals. Did that stop a guy from coming to my house and telling me he's allergic to dogs? No, but I did quickly escort him out the door. I also once dated a man who turned out to be a religious zealot. When he said I was a pagan and could never understand him, I added "religious zealots" to my list of deal-breakers. Other things I added to my list: men who were unemployed, men with children, and those who didn't want to ever get married.

Once you make your own list of deal-breakers, learn how to ask questions to get real answers, and then make plans accordingly. Why? So you don't waste your time!

When it comes to relationships, remember this: it is important to ask questions in such a way that a potential partner does not know the answer you are looking for—in case they are one of those who will just tell you what you want to hear. As for your parents' infirmities, do you think nursing homes are deal-breakers? If so, you need to prepare a space in your home and plan for the finances to afford an in-home caretaker. What are your deal-breakers about educating your children? What are your deal-breakers in terms of changing your career path?

In searching for my own life partner, it took me several years of trial and error, just saying "No," and walking away. People often ask how Robby and I met. It was April of 2001, at a restaurant called BJ's, which served the most delicious blackened salmon and was right across the street from my office in Los Angeles. I knew that executives from the *CSI* television series gathered there after the day's shooting. I had not been dating for a while, but now I was ready to meet someone. A TV executive might be interesting! This was my plan: I would go in at three in the afternoon, after the executives would have wrapped up filming. My plan was to sit at the bar, have a drink, and pretend I was interested in watching the televised sports. As I walked in, I noticed an interesting-looking man wearing a red Ferrari Formula One jacket and sitting alone at the bar. I was driving a black Corvette at the time, and racing was in my heart. I took a seat with only one empty stool between us, and after ordering a drink, I broke the ice by turning to him and asking him about his jacket. I then went on to ask about his job. (I wanted someone who was passionate about their work.) I asked if he was currently married. (I had never been married.) Did he have any children? (I live my life child-free.) What place of worship did he attend? (I am totally open-minded about religion, except for zealots.) Was he a Democrat or a Republican? (I didn't want to fight about politics.) I had a few more deal-breaking questions for him, and after he answered all my inquiries the way I had visualized them being answered, I lived with him for several years and then married him. And no, he was not one of the *CSI* film executives.

Manage Your Curveballs

There were no deal-breakers in the beginning of our relationship, and there still aren't any today. But even so, those first few months were hard, very hard, and required a commitment on both of our parts to get to know and accept each other's needs and what we wanted from a relationship. Of course, life never goes exactly according to plan, even if you are a most conscientious planner like me. And people are unpredictable, which means life, and relationships in particular, will throw you curveballs. Robby and I struggled with the fact that we had both been totally independent and not reliant on anyone for a long time. That was not a deal-breaker, but it nevertheless created challenges. We decided to separate for a time. I stayed in California, and he went to New York City, and then he planned on going to his mother's place in Florida. He was at his mother's when 9/11 hit, and that event changed everything.

I called him that fateful morning, not knowing if he was still in New York City or what had just happened.

But whatever it was, I told him I did not want to face it alone. Robby got into his truck and drove for three days, back into my arms. We have now been together for twenty years, and I've loved every minute of it. Well, almost every minute, since no one, including Robby, is perfect. But I have no doubt that Robby and I will be lifelong partners.

In planning my life goals, I had known that getting to the next level in my career, while also enjoying a fulfilling personal life, would require help. I would need a partner to share my life and help me with the journey. I had also learned that life gets more complicated as you age. You have more friends who need you. You have family that relies on you. You have a job or career that takes up time. Robby retired early from his nine-to-five job and now has a full-time, twenty-four-seven job taking care of me, our home, and the demands of our different properties. He loves to take care of everything with a motor, and he provides me with the comfort of knowing that all household projects are being handled, so I can concentrate on my work. In exchange, I handle all the budgeting, planning, and home office work—basically all the financial matters. We know each other's strengths and weaknesses, and it works. In Chapter 7, I discuss matching a team member's skills to the job. It works at home as well. When you know each other's strengths, you can assign tasks to whichever partner would handle them better. As Robby says, "Nora, you're the engine in our lives. I'm the mechanic."

So yes, Robby fit the bill as a partner to help me manage my life. But 9/11 also taught me I needed a partner to do so much more. I learned that owning your life includes finding a way to handle those things you cannot control. And I learned that those things that had been troubling me when we separated were immaterial compared to having someone to help me deal with the curveballs, great and small, that I would invariably face throughout the rest of my life.

My youngest brother, Wally, was not so fortunate after 9/11. He could not get over the images of bodies falling from the Twin Towers, and barely five months later, on February 3, 2002, at the age of twenty-five, he repeated their journey. He drove into Boston from his hometown in New Hampshire, checked into a high-rise hotel, and jumped from the twenty-fifth floor. I have never understood how one event could have affected so many lives; Robby says it's the butterfly effect. One action of a crazed man from a cave in the Middle East, and all our lives are changed forever. I miss my brother every single day and only wish he could have visualized a healthy future for himself.

Seize Control

If I had not found a life partner that had none of the deal-breakers on my list, I still would have been happy to live life alone. I have been studying family dynamics since I started handling family estates at the age of eighteen, and I've seen way too many horrible first marriages that inevitably ended in divorce and pain. Along the way, I made the conscious decision to skip the possibility of divorce and remarriage and instead to wait until I was ready and had found the right partner.

I have been truly fortunate that things worked out as intended, and now my first marriage is equivalent to most people's second (or third) marriage. But doesn't everyone have those expectations—that the first marriage will work out? Yes, but then life happens. What made my situation different was two things: First, I was patient. Because I was older than most women are when they get married, I was able to take those vows— for better or worse, for richer or poorer, in sickness and in health—more seriously than I might have when I was younger. And second, as Robby and I face challenges together, we have held the belief that marriage is very much a contract, and as with a business contract, each side *must* hold up their end of the bargain.

Visualizing the outcome will help you recognize opportunities and help seize control of them when they arise. For example, if your boss makes a sexist remark—and most of the time they don't even realize it's sexist—you should seize control and take the opportunity to speak up. Walk out of meetings when men repeatedly interrupt and talk over you. Put an end to phone calls when the other person refuses to hear what you have to say. I know this can be easier said than done; women often do not feel comfortable reacting instantly. We like to think about what we *should* have said. We dream about how we could have stomped out of a meeting to make a point. We regret not being able to just hang up on an abusive caller. My advice is this: Stop dreaming and stop wishing. Start taking action and seize control of your life. The more you do this, the easier it becomes. Trust me: the people in the room will remember your actions and think twice the next time they want to play their silly little games.

It has been in those moments when I have had no control that I've learned I must act instantly, especially when I needed to act for the safety of my person and the business I've built over years of hard work. Over a decade ago, I was the only woman in a conference room full of colleagues for our office's weekly sales meeting when one of the men blocked the door, locking us all in. He then threatened to kill us all if the manager did not help him with some issue. I don't even remember what the issue was; what I do recall is looking to the left and then to the right and seeing panic on the faces of my male colleagues as we all realized the only exit was through the door he was blocking. Although I did not see a gun, I had been in offices with fights and even shootings before, so I knew how this could end. The manager made it worse by asking the man blocking the door if he was taking his meds. Eventually, the two men in the room that were the closest to him talked him down and escorted him out of the conference room.

Friends have asked what happened to the guy. Was he fired? Was he prosecuted? No. He made the firm too much money. The firm's solution was to keep him on the payroll but to contain the lunacy. In fact, the only action taken was that the human resources department told him he was not allowed out of his office except according to a schedule when he could go to the bathroom. But that was not good enough for me: enough is enough; it was time to take action. I marched into my manager's office and demanded a safe place to work, and I put into writing, in a memo to the president, that I would be working from home until 50 percent of the managers and workers in the office were women, not counting the 99 percent female support staff. In retrospect, I guess my thinking was that an office with more women in positions of control would make it a safer environment. But more important, I knew from experience that that personnel shift would never happen, and therefore, I would have a valid reason to never go into that office again. Fortunately, I was making enough money for the firm that, just like the guy with issues, they could not afford to fire me. I quickly found how much I truly loved my decision and the actions I took. I no longer had to try to be *one of the guys* or go to my male-designed, dark-wood, square office. And I was much, much safer.

Seizing control is important in all aspects of life, not just in those life-threatening circumstances. Whenever I have a meeting, I take control by preparing a structured agenda. I know what I want to say, I am as prepared as a porcupine for any objections, and I keep the meetings from going offtrack. I also control my own space and time, which means that when someone else calls a meeting, I ask for their agenda in advance. If they don't have one, I know it will be a waste of my time, and I don't attend.

On a broader basis, I control my day as if it were an interactive play. I have the opening sequence (my morning), and I choose which actors I will interact with (team members, clients, friends, and family). And then I both watch and participate in the performance in ensuing sequences—performances that inspire me.

Sure, I want surprises and thrills, but I also want security and peace. Sometimes I even have to fire actors who detract from my main story line. In the last chapter, Chapter 11, I give you a look into my life and more about how I structure my day.

Just so you know I'm being honest with myself, let me tell you that, even with all the seizing control and visualizing that I do, I don't know if I've "made it." I assume I may never know. Life is the journey of trying to find that out. But if I refer back to my definition of happiness—finding peace with myself and the life I've created—I can honestly say that, at least on most days, the answer is a resounding, "Yes! I have indeed found happiness."

Of course, there will always be paths I did not take that I reminisce about from time to time. I should have stuck with my Apple stock. I should have started my own hedge fund. I should have written this book years ago. But life does not come with twenty-twenty sight, and it seldom allows do-overs. The point I'm making here is that I have control of my life, and I want to help you take control over yours too. When I'm asked, "Why do you do what you do?" I explain that I do it because of the challenge. My industry has its problems, but I still love it. My job throws obstacles in my path, and some clients stress me out. But I do what I do because I've learned how to be in control of my life: I decide what I do, where I do it, and with whom.

CHAPTER THREE

ACCEPT BOTH NATURE AND NURTURE

If you're not failing, you're not pushing your limits, and if you're not pushing your limits, you're not maximizing your potential.

—Ray Dalio, *Principles: Life and Work*

L et's take a chapter and explore what defines us. One of the oldest existential debates is that of nature versus nurture. Are you more defined by your DNA or by your environment? Which drives you to work hard? Which will better guarantee success? Which offers a life of happiness?

Embrace the Duality

Few people know that I was born in Venezuela. At the age of six, I came to the United States with my brother Ivan, my American mother, and my Venezuelan stepfather. My biological Venezuelan father and my mother had divorced when I was born. Just to clarify, my brother Wally, whom I talked about earlier, was a half brother; he was born in the US after we arrived.

I did not know a lick of English, and I certainly had never seen snow when we settled in a town of four hundred souls in the mountains of New England. It was quite a change after living with millions in Caracas, the capital of Venezuela, where my brother and I first learned that what we were born into was not the same as how the world saw us. For example, although we were not poor, we would smear dirt on our faces and then beg for money so we could buy candy. When we came to Mont Vernon, New Hampshire, the townspeople got together and gave us clothes. They assumed we were poor because we hailed from Latin America. We were not poor, but we sure loved their kindness. And although Ivan and I quickly learned English and did well in school, we successfully fooled the teachers and other kids by acting like we did not understand English. We spoke to each other in Spanish, and although the other kids basically treated us like aliens who had landed on their planet, it was great fun! Like so many immigrants, we had come to America with our ingrained desire to succeed and enjoy life, and we were soon overwhelmed with the freedom and expansive options that life in America offered versus life in Venezuela—this was the "nurture" part of our lives.

Our nature was to learn and succeed, and the nurture part—the opportunities that living in America offered—served us well. Ivan graduated from Dartmouth College, knowing exactly what he wanted to do—become a physician. Today, he has a successful concierge medical practice in Winter Park, Florida. I graduated from USC and, as I wrote about in Chapter 1, found my career early on as well. How did we do that? In addition to our natural desire to learn, the nurture side of the equation involved the influence of two key people in our lives. The first was our biological father, a university professor and poet, whom we spent time with in Venezuela whenever we could. On one of his visits to the States, my father presented Robby's mother with a book of his poetry, written in Spanish. Since she could not read it, she later asked me in private about the subject matter of my father's poetry. "Oh," I replied. "Dark and sexual." That was my father: a warm, wonderful, and very Latin man who stressed education.

The other person who influenced our lives was our uncle, Don Howarth. Don graduated from Harvard University and became the youngest partner at a Los

Angeles law firm. We visited him several times while we were growing up, and seeing his life there was why I chose USC. The influence of those two men was the foundation for why my brother and I are where we are today. Without them I doubt we could have ever imagined life outside that small New Hampshire town.

But not all influences in life are good—genetic or environmental. My stepfather's contribution, which also falls on the nurture side of the equation, was a decade of sexual abuse. From the age of six to seventeen (when I could finally get the hell out of the house), my stepfather made my life miserable. Friends and those helping me put this book together suggested it would be good therapy for me to expand on and detail here exactly the abuse that happened. I disagree. I've dealt with the trauma with a therapist; in my own way, I've now put it behind me and will leave it there. Let me simply say I took all that anger and focused it into getting good grades, which then created the opportunity for me to earn a full academic scholarship, get on a plane, and head off to college at the age of seventeen, leaving my circumstances behind. I never looked back.

I will admit that that anger still drives me today. For those of you who have been in similar circumstances, know that you have a choice. You can either let the anger consume you and drive you to self-destruct, or you can channel it to move on. I chose the latter, and you can too. If your experience has been like mine, I recommend you read a book that was referred to me by a friend a few years ago: *The Body Keeps the Score: Brain, Mind, and Body in the Healing of Trauma* by Bessel van der Kolk, MD. Reading it helped me understand and deal with the lingering trauma from that devastating experience that I know will be with me my entire life.

Fortunately, early on after leaving home, I knew that to be successful, I had to get control of my life. I also knew I had to create a safe environment where I could grow and nurture the person I hoped—and knew—I could become. Quite frankly, I don't know how I knew this; I just did. So was it nature (my genetic gene pool) or nurture (which included both opportunity and a tragic home life) that was responsible for who I have become? I can only believe it's a combination of both, a blend of the bad with the good. What I do know, without a doubt, is that getting control over my life was so important to me that spreading that message, and providing others with the tools to accomplish it, was a major motivating factor in deciding to write this book.

Know Your Options

Once you recognize that both nature and nurture influence your life's path, it's vitally important to know that you are never stuck—you always have options. This is so important, and I will stress it repeatedly throughout the book. When I meet with clients and young people seeking advice, I always let them know they have options, and the more options they have, the better. Once they embrace this idea, I can help them explore what those options are and how to pursue them, keeping in mind that no matter how bad or hopeless their situation may seem, *walking away and starting over* is always an option.

Turn Dreams into Goals

One of life's magical wonders, which few people ever learn, is that dreams become goals with a plan. For me, life holds no greater reward than knowing I have helped others understand that their dreams can come true, and also knowing I have helped make that happen. It does not matter how you were born (*nature*) or the circumstances you faced in getting to this point in life (*nurture*). It only matters that you know who you are and where you are today. With that knowledge you can make your dreams come true with a plan. And that is where I can help.

When I interview and first get to know new clients as fellow human beings struggling to make their lives meaningful, I start by ascertaining their objectives and goals in life. It is only with this information that I can help guide them along their life's journey and know how to manage their money to make their desires possible.

A simple fact is that having more money provides you with more options. It's also a fact that understanding your financial situation provides you with more options, since you then have the ability to plan realistically. You would be surprised how few people are aware of these basic facts. Once I have provided my clients with this knowledge, I am then able to assist them in developing and executing a plan to accomplish and achieve their dreams. In other words, I help them move from how they are living today to creating their *authentic* lives. It's not easy. It takes hard work, perseverance, and maintaining a positive attitude while enduring setbacks and failures. But it is doable. One of the reasons I have such a high success rate in obtaining new clients, and keeping my current ones, is that I am very good at what I do. There is a saying: *Everything is easy when you know what to do.* And you only know what to do when you've done it many times before. I have done this many times with many clients!

Michelle was forty-four when I first met her in Los Angeles. She was referred to me by her psychologist after an ugly divorce. Married since she was twenty, she was now feeling emotionally insecure and scared, and she had two angry teenagers to take care of. Fortunately, she had negotiated a large settlement and came to me to manage it. Even with the settlement, after years of being told she was worthless, stupid, and needed to work, she had no idea how she was going to survive and make ends meet financially. She had a nursing background, and before I met her, she had quickly jumped at an emergency-room nursing position, which turned into an eighty-hour workweek that left her vulnerable teenagers alone at home. This is not uncommon; I had seen this scenario a number of times. In a situation like Michelle's, the first thing is not to explore her dreams and goals. The first thing is to teach her how to budget. Once we had a budget in hand, I was then able to prove to her that she had options and that she did not need to take such an exhausting and time-consuming position to the detriment of her children, who would be home for only a few more years. With a budget in hand, she could confidently change her job to one with reasonable hours so she could be there when they arrived home from school. And that is exactly what she did by taking a part-time job in a nearby doctor's office.

I then began the task of exploring with her, over the ensuing months and years, what her ideal life might look like. I did this by asking a series of questions: What would make you feel safe and secure? What do you want to accomplish in life? How would you describe your *authentic* life—that place where you are in control and happiest? We explored her various options in each important aspect of her life.

The first area we explored was the question of how she could support her children and pay for their education. We worked out a financial plan so they could go to college, which both did, without having to take part-time jobs or be burdened with huge student loans. (Although in Michelle's case it was not financially necessary, at my suggestion, we did leave them with small student loans to help them learn financial responsibility and how to handle money.) After graduation, both joined the United States Coast Guard and now have very successful careers. Another issue we looked at was Michelle's passions. At the top of that list was a love of horses, something not compatible with her life in Los Angeles. So we talked about how and where she might be able to pursue her equestrian interests. And of course we also discussed relationships. Michelle had been dating a man from South Carolina and had fallen in love with him and the rural, countryside lifestyle he led there. When she told me she wanted to move in with him and live there, I asked the critical question I believe is imperative for all women to ask at this point in a relationship: If this man were not in your life, would this still feel like the right move? Would it still feel authentic to you? The question I faced Michelle with was, "Can you find peace and happiness being alone in a remote, rural town if the relationship doesn't work?" I did not let her answer right away. I told her to think about it over the next week and then let me know. One week to the day later, she called. "Yes," she said. "That is the kind of life I want to lead."

We then embarked on creating a plan, both financial and otherwise, about how and when she would move to South Carolina once the kids went off to college. There, she would be able to live on a ranch with her beloved horses and, if all worked out right, start a life with her new partner. She did it. And even though, as happens all too often, the relationship fell apart shortly after her move, she was okay. She called to commiserate, and we cried together for an hour, and then she said, "Nora, I no longer feel stupid and insecure. This move was the right decision. I can't thank you enough for guiding me here."

I had known all along that she had the innate stamina, grit, and courage to rebuild her life. That is, she had the right *nature*. And even though the *nurture* part of her life, especially her failed marriage, had involved a lot of suffering, causing her to lose confidence in herself in a way similar to how my personal experience of abuse had caused my own pain, she—like me—was able to channel her discomfort from those years into a positive direction once she understood that she had options. We talk often nowadays, and she has never been happier. To me, Michelle is the ideal client. While I am primarily responsible for managing her money, the personal relationship we have developed, and the knowledge that I am able to help her plan and achieve what she wants out of life, are what give me the most satisfaction. Tell me: How many male financial planners think of their relationships with their clients as I do? I'm sure there are a handful, but I also believe that building these types of relationships is more in a woman's basic nature than a man's—yet another way that *nature* can factor into what we do in our lives.

Have a Flexible Plan B

Earlier I mentioned the importance of knowing your options. One of those options should be to always have a fallback Plan B. I always felt that if I failed at my career, my Plan B would be to go back to Venezuela and restart my life there. But in 2010, when I returned to Venezuela for my father's eightieth birthday, I realized the homeland I loved so much had now become a mere shadow of the once powerful, rich, and democratically free country that I had known while growing up. Disguised as a Democrat, Hugo Chávez had become a corrupt dictator of Venezuela in 1999, and over a short number of years, he destroyed the dreams of millions. My Venezuelan family became destitute, along with countless other families. To this day, Nicolás Maduro, who came after Chávez, runs Venezuela in such a way that it has become just a faint whisper of the great country it once was. Rolling blackouts cripple a country drowning in its own petroleum, and the once vibrant middle class has become nonexistent, totally dependent on the so-called benevolent government just to survive. During my last visit there, I was afraid to even walk to the corner for fear of being robbed of my cell phone and shoes, and two of my half brothers, still living in Caracas, had been kidnapped for ransom more than once. This was not a country I recognized or could be proud of, and it had happened so quickly. When Robby and I returned from our trip and I saw the American flag out the cabin window as the plane landed in Miami, joyful tears streamed down my face.

My Plan B was no longer one of my options, but here in America I had a home. A place that was free and secure. I almost kissed the stained airport carpet out of appreciation once I cleared customs. I was like all the immigrants before me that have landed in this country. You cherish the ability to express yourself in any way you want without the threat of being taken away at night. My own Venezuelan stepmother was living under the threat of being jailed for her subversive writings against the government. One of my Venezuelan half brothers was, and still is, hiding in Spain from the threat of retribution from a president who is scared of free speech. In the US, one has the right to seek recourse for wrongs through our judicial system—not a perfect system, but a system nonetheless. You have the freedom to walk down the street, to drive in your car, and to surf the internet without government intervention. A person never appreciates this until it's taken away. And, with unbelievable gratitude,

I cried for having this country to come home to. I challenge you to go for a few weeks to a foreign, restrictive country, have the air sucked out of you, and not totally understand why the people don't revolt against these political machines. Think about the Arab Spring in 2011. And Tiananmen Square thirty years ago. The fight goes on.

Before my Plan B imploded, I had felt I could take risks with my career and my investments and always fall back on what I assumed would be an equally wonderful but vastly different life in my home country. I once even considered getting a business partner so I could spend three months a year in Venezuela. When my Plan B was erased during my last trip there, I saw that I needed to take action to realign my life. Fortunately, I had become successful enough in my chosen career that my new Plan B was to start my own financial services company and operate independently, under the umbrella of a large firm. I also now help Venezuelan immigrants integrate into our culture and start their new lives here in America. I will tell you more about that in Chapter 9.

Remember, no matter how helpless, hopeless, or miserable a situation may seem—and whether it stems from your biological background or the world that surrounds you—you always have options. And, as I said earlier, walking away and starting over is always one of those options. For me, walking away from my long-standing Plan B was the choice I made.

CHAPTER FOUR

GET TO KNOW—AND BE COMFORTABLE WITH—YOURSELF

The key to your happiness is to own your slippers, own who you are, own how you look, own your family, own the talents you have, and own the ones you don't. If you keep saying your slippers are not yours, then you'll die searching, you'll die bitter, always feeling you were promised more. Not only our actions, but also our omissions, become your destiny.

—Abraham Verghese, *Cutting for Stone*

Now we get to another important issue—getting to know and becoming comfortable with yourself. It's important to find a career or job that identifies with your strengths and values, but it's even more important that your personal life reflects them. The secret is to get to a place of peace. Some people meditate; some people do yoga. Some get on their bikes or climb rocks. Some go to the gym. My place of peace is my eighty-five-degree pool, where I listen to my favorite music and think about what ultimately makes me content. Only then can I listen to my innermost self.

Create Space for Yourself

Wherever and however you do it, think about your day. Was it successful? Did you accomplish what you wanted and needed to do? How about tomorrow—how is it lining up? I make this time a required habit when I rejoice in my accomplishments and daydream about upcoming trips. I think about the last book I read or movie I watched. I strategically think about difficult topics that are outside my comfort zone, like how to deal with IRS audits and upcoming litigation. And then I swim off the frustrations and matters that I can't fix right now.

It's also a time and a place to dream. I make sure I spend at least thirty minutes each day doing exactly that. When clients tell me they don't have thirty minutes to dream, I tell them to *schedule it*. Make it a priority, and tell your family this is *your* time. Hang up a Do Not Disturb sign if you have to. Time to dream is critically important; we all need it—not just when we are sleeping but also when we are most awake and in touch with our inner selves. The next day will be when you work on the plan to make those dreams come true. But first, you must have time to be creative and come up with the dreams in the first place. Time just to *think* is perhaps the most important time of the entire day. And when you schedule and take that time, your life will reflect your authentic self because you will have outlined it over and over again and chosen what gives you peace, comfort, and happiness. Trust me—and do it.

Get Organized

It is essential that you keep your day organized. I can't tell you how many times I've called a client only to be told they are too busy to call me back, to sign a document, or even to breathe. No one is that busy. They are simply disorganized. Organization is the key to efficiency. If you start your day looking for your keys, your files, your accessories, or milk for your coffee, face the fact: you are disorganized.

Since my goal in writing this book is to help make your life better, let me tell you how to get organized. Start by making a commitment to yourself to organize one area of your home or office every week. Organize your jewelry and accessories in drawers so they are easy to see. Go through your makeup and hair products and get rid of those that have expired or that you've never used. And don't tell me you don't have any of those; every woman does. Arrange your closet so you can easily find outfits for work or social events. Set up your pantry and fridge so you can find ingredients, and throw out expired items once a month. Systemize your projects into separate folders or email files for easy access to data. Use a day-timer system of some kind to keep track of your daily, weekly, and monthly goals. Stagger your cleaning duties during the week so you don't waste an entire weekend day doing all the laundry and vacuuming. Arrange your garage shelves by hobby, so you can easily find the items you need when it's time to have fun. Keep your car clean and tidy in case you need to give someone a ride after lunch, or just to feel good about yourself. If you don't have bandwidth in your day—and nothing devours bandwidth like disorganization—you will never get beyond where you are. You will have reached your capacity and be unable to take on new tasks. You will be stuck.

There is a saying that *work expands to fill the time available*. This is oh so true. And if you are filling your time with busywork or are inefficient, you will never become more productive. I see men in their offices till ten at night and on weekends. That does not make them more successful than me. Often, they are playing a part to make themselves look good to some senior manager, or they are disorganized to the point that they cannot complete their job in eight hours—or, even worse, they don't want to go home because they have a dismal personal life.

To make yourself valuable to the business for which you work, show up on time and have outstanding work product. It's not how many hours you put into a project but rather the efficacy of how you perform on that project. And when you get organized, you will become more proactive and in control of your daily routine. You will no longer simply be reacting to everything that crosses your path, and you will have more time and space to think and be creative.

Evaluate Your Work/Life Balance

Becoming comfortable with yourself demands a work/life balance that meets your needs. Unfortunately, I have often seen how challenging that can be for clients who have a difficult home life; the balancing act then becomes an ongoing struggle. If you have a personal life fraught with drama, it will affect your work performance. Conversely, if you have a job that makes you frustrated, it will affect your personal relationships.

Remember, you always have options. And one of those options is to continuously evaluate your work/life balance and make course adjustments when necessary. Change is never easy, but it will often benefit everyone involved. One of the most common things I have heard clients or friends tell me is that they are only staying in their relationship because of the kids. My reply is always the same. "Don't you think the kids know you're miserable? If you are unhappy, they must be unhappy too. The best thing you can do for the kids is to not stay in the relationship as it is, but instead change it or get out. Everyone will be happier—including the kids." I then offer to work with them to make a plan to do just that.

Celebrate Yourself

A wise woman once told me, "You will never be as young or as thin as you are right now." Let that sink in. I have known clients who were dieting on their death-bed. Make peace with your body and treat it right, and you will live a longer and more fulfilling life than one in which you spend too much time hoping and failing to achieve an imagined persona. While your longevity depends somewhat on your genes, self-kindness is also an immensely powerful component. An excellent book on this topic is *Lifespan: Why We Age—and Why We Don't Have To*, by David A. Sinclair, PhD. He provides some great tools to accomplish what I have outlined.

Along the same lines, choose a partner who loves you as you are, not as you might be. The journey, not the destination, must be the fun part of a relation-ship. Whether it be in business or with a marriage, the goal is to never reach a final destination—unless that destination is a decision that the relationship is over, and I've never known anyone who sets that as a goal. The goal is to always have another thumbtack in the map of life, another journey. That is the map of a good marriage and a good business model, and it's only possible if you have a partner who isn't always trying to change you.

Celebrate your wins! Whether it's landing a new client or organizing your pantry, it's a success you should own and be proud of. When you accomplish a goal, gift yourself with presents and then pick out a new destination on your journey. Unless you have a truly amazing partner, no one else will do it for you!

Revel in your steadfastness, your resolve, and your adaptability, because life is going to throw you some ugly curveballs. Don't let what life throws at you define you. It's not what happens to you in life; it's how you adapt and recover.

Be patient with your journey. If you are like me, until you hit forty you will strive to figure out your destinations without even knowing what the map looks like. I recommend that, no matter your age, you read *The Subtle Art of Not Giving a F*ck* by Mark Manson. He tells the whys and hows of what I'm writing about in this chapter as well as anyone I have read.

It took me until I was forty to begin learning the process of merging my authentic self with the image I had become so good at projecting to others. I learned, for example, that I had leeches in my life who needed to be thrown out. Some were people who had been around me for a long time and that I called friends, but they no longer added value to my life. When they began coveting my life and discouraging me from taking risks, and when they were not on their own learning journeys, I knew I needed to get them out of my life and come up with a new definition of *friend*.

As life goes on and mortality starts rearing its ugly head, you will discover that time is your most valuable commodity. You will not have time for leeches or friends who suck the energy out of your life with their never-ending drama and negativity. By the time I was fifty, it was *look out, world!* That's when I simply stopped caring what others might think. I had to own my life. I made peace with what I had accomplished, and I invited people into my life that were going to reflect that.

The masks you wear when you are younger can become exhausting. For years I believed that I had to wear the mask of a perfectionist. I had to wear the mask of toughness, to prove that all those office humiliations did not affect me. I wore the mask of neutrality when I listened to clients and friends tell me their skewed side of a damaging relationship, even when I knew they shared at least part of the guilt. I wore the mask of a person filled with confidence, when in fact my insecurities were abundant. Not anymore. I no longer wear masks. I am my true self: an ever-changing, flawed, progress junkie who is always looking and moving ahead, who loves life's adventures, and who has accumulated a variety of friends from many walks of life. And while I'm not in a rush to get there, I know it's going to be extremely interesting to see how I evolve in later decades. I am not afraid; I am curious.

Anticipate the Crossroads

It's not unusual to come to a crossroads in life and not know which direction to turn. Too many people become paralyzed. Their decision-making skills may be faulty, or perhaps their past experiences confirm their inability to see the opportunities and dangers that lie ahead. Their negative self-talk may be unceasing, or their own inner leech voices tell them not to take either road. When a person is stuck at a crossroads, they might not know whether to listen to their head, their heart, or their gut. If that person is you, let me help by giving you some insights and tools on how to choose the road to take with confidence.

I have encountered many crossroads, and I will admit it can be terrifying to make major decisions, such as getting out of a marriage, moving across states, having children, managing affairs after the death of a parent, or choosing among alternatives when facing a critical illness. It's always frightening to think that the direction you take will not be the right one. Let me tell you how I handle these types of decisions: I ask my good friends for their valuable input. I read and study authors who have gone down the same road. I make a list of pros and cons. I discuss options with my husband. I think about the choices during my swims. It is only then, after I have looked at all the data available, that I choose a direction.

But know that it's not enough just to take the time to evaluate the alternatives; you must also be willing to take risks outside your comfort zone. If possible, try on, even wear, a decision for a while. And if it turns out not to be the correct course, then reevaluate the data, readjust, and change course. That's life. The most important thing is that you make a decision, remembering that it's seldom a decision between *good* and *bad*. Most decisions are between *good* and *maybe a little better*, and good is always a better choice than no decision at all. What most people fail to realize is that no decision is a decision in itself, and one that almost always leads to frustration and remorse about what *could have been*.

I remember going through this process about fifteen years ago, when we were contemplating a move from Los Angeles to Las Vegas. I just could not visualize making the move. I had arrived in Los Angeles at age seventeen and grown up there. I had learned about life in that ruthless city. But I had been there for twenty years and had explored everything there was to do in California. I was tired of the traffic that seemed to consume at least a third of my life. And the taxes never stopped mounting. Yet I was reluctant to leave, in part because I had only recently met my husband-to-be, who had also spent the last twenty years in that city.

But Robby's mother had been dating a man in Las Vegas, and when we went to visit them, we discovered a Las Vegas that was completely different from the city it had been years earlier when I had hung out at Circus Circus. It had become an adult playground, and Robby and I had a blast exploring all the dining options, the shopping, and the never-ending opportunities for concerts and shows. We looked at each other and had the same thought: we wanted to live there. That was the decision. But before making the move, I knew I had to evaluate all current data and make sure I was taking the right path. I conferred with friends, spoke with clients, and visited Las Vegas a few more times. I made my list of pros and cons. What probably sealed the deal was the fact that our projected savings on state taxes alone would cover our entire mortgage and essentially give us a free home. Yay! I could easily hop on a Southwest Airlines flight for fifty dollars to see my clients back in Los Angeles in less than an hour—yay! And clients located in other cities would be happy to visit me in Las Vegas. Yay again! I could explore a totally new state, too, and feel like a tourist once again.

Even with all the overwhelming reasons to support our decision to move, the dilemma haunted my nights as I wondered what we were doing—and why. Major decisions are often hard to make; the answers lie in the pros and cons and how much each weighs in terms of relative importance. In the end, the pros for moving to Las Vegas won. We made the move, and I had never been happier. You see, I have long known that once a decision is made, you must own it. Don't second-guess it—embrace it. That will help the outcome be what you had visualized. For Robby and me, that meant exploring everything there was to do around town, as well as going on weekend treks to Utah. Then one day, ten years later, we looked at each other and knew it was time for another change—Texas. Robby had turned fifty and asked me to go home with him. He is a tenth-generation Texan, and every Texan I have ever known eventually returns home. So I had to start the decision-making process all over again, although I was sure of the result even before starting.

Identify Your Destination

We face crossroads throughout our lives, especially as we try to navigate direction. As you know by now, I don't simply help my clients make financial decisions. A major part of what I do is help them find their way by answering the question: *Is what I'm doing, or where I'm going, OK?* Is it OK to retire? Is it OK to fly-fish every day? Is it OK to work at a nonprofit for nothing? Is it OK to go see the pandas in China? I encourage clients to share their dreams and secrets with me, because that is what creates bonds between people—especially between women. How wonderful is it to be able to talk about your vulnerabilities and your aspirations with someone who truly cares and is not judgmental? That is the person I strive to be for my clients as well as my friends. Whatever their next destination might be, my job is to help them find a way to get there, which of course includes helping them find a way to afford it. My reward is then to go along for the ride.

Lauren had come to me as a single woman with the dream of becoming an actor. In Los Angeles this is, of course, a common goal that often does not have a happy ending. Hollywood loves young, beautiful ingénues, and there is such a small window of time to succeed as an actress, but once you pass a certain age, the window closes quickly. It's only then that women realize they spent their early years, when they had the most energy and enthusiasm for life, chasing an unattainable dream while bartending or doing banal office work. This is not just a problem for women in Los Angeles; it's true for any gender in cities and towns around the world. It's especially true for those looking for fame in professions such as acting, music, or sports. The drive to overcome nearly impossible hurdles can consume years, but I would never advise anyone *not* to chase their dreams. My goal is to help make those dreams come true, but to also always ensure that they have a Plan B.

Lauren worked as a receptionist at a law firm while she waited for her big break. She came to me because her parents had died and left her a moderate inheritance. In our conversations, she confided in me that she was obsessed with the Panda Cams at the Smithsonian's National Zoo. She watched the giant pandas on the cameras from work and at home, and she regaled me with stories about what the pandas did.

I asked, "So why don't you visit the pandas in China, their native land?"

Her immediate response was to ask me if she could afford it.

"You can if we budget for it," I told her.

And that's what we did. A dream had become a goal, and Lauren returned from her trip to see the pandas in China a changed woman. We then made plans and a budget for her to go on an African safari the next year.

As for her acting career? Lauren didn't make it. But she did become a paralegal focused on working with the LGBTQ+ community. That was her Plan B that we had worked out together. If she couldn't be an actor, being a paralegal would provide her with a lifestyle that she would enjoy, which now includes visiting animal reserves around the world on a budget that allows it. You see, since talk is cheap, I go one step—and often several steps—further to help my clients create and plan how to achieve their Plan B and enjoy a lifestyle of their dreams, even if it's a second choice. That's what I do for myself, and it's what I do for my clients. It's also what you need to do for yourself. As for me, think how exciting and wonderful it is to be able to help make someone else's life better and share their adventures! Try being there for your friends and families in the same way. The most important thing is not to be jealous of what they have or are able to do. Ask questions, share secrets, support their journey, and savor the moments. Doing so will make your life immeasurably better.

Leave It at the Office

One of the primary pieces of advice I offer clients who are learning how to become comfortable with themselves is this: *Leave it at the office.* To be happy with yourself, you must learn to divest yourself of negative feelings, especially those arising from a hostile work environment. When I fail to let it go, Robby calls it *redundant anger.* Really, how many times can I be mad at the way my industry operates? How many times can I be mad at the petty slights or just the sheer ignorance of how a woman is treated? The answer is: a lot! But I absolutely must leave all this redundant anger behind when I get home. It's not fair to my husband, to my family, or to my friends. Perhaps most important, it's not fair to me. If I don't learn to leave it behind, it makes me ugly and unappreciative of what I have and what I have accomplished. And taking it out on a spouse or a friend is simply wrong.

I have a male friend, a very successful lawyer, who has been divorced three times and is afraid he will die alone. Recently he told me his latest dating woes; his girlfriend had just left him. He'd had a terrible day in court, and he had yelled at her when he arrived home, spoiling a special occasion. Sadly, he had told me a similar story before.

I finally had to ask him, "Is that how you treat your clients and the people who are important to you at your firm?"

"Of course not," he replied. "I would never do that."

"So why would you treat your girlfriend and potential life partner that way? Shouldn't she be the most important person in your life? Doesn't she deserve the same respect, patience, and focus you give to your clientele?"

Knowing, and being comfortable with, ourselves means being able to separate our work lives from our home lives. It's not just a matter of balance between the two, which I touched on earlier. It's also recognizing that each of these two parts of our lives uses very different skill sets and also impacts our mindsets differently. When we understand this, and when we can accept that one part of our lives might be more of a struggle than the other on any given day, we will more readily find the happiness and stability we seek in our other relationships. To put it more simply, it's wrong to make our spouses, families, or friends be the receptacle of our office frustrations.

Design Your Own Environment

Owning your own life is easier said than done. One of the greatest challenges I faced in the male-dominated corporate world was learning to accept who I was and to stand up for myself. I found myself spending a huge amount of time and energy dealing with toxic environments. It was not enough that I had to work in a depressing physical office with ugly furniture and drab, depressing carpets. I also had to put up with the sexist jokes, the strippers for all the guys' birthdays, and being treated like I was invisible when I offered any suggestions. Over time I discovered several workable strategies I could use to set myself up for success if I wanted to be recognized—and if I wanted to be happy. Let me tell you about a few, with the hope that you'll give them a try, modifying them as necessary to fit whatever toxic circumstances you might face.

First and foremost, create your own work space and environment. We have already talked about the importance of setting up a time and space for personal contemplation. We have also talked about organizing your physical space so you don't waste time. Now it's time to think about your environment, both at the office and at home, in terms of what makes you happy and how it reflects who *you* are. Add fresh flowers and use reed diffusers to make your work space look and smell wonderful. Place a beautiful rug over the ugly corporate carpet or linoleum floor. Use gorgeous lamps rather than fluorescent bulbs. Fill your office with beautiful file folders, colorful pens, and anything else that makes it look and feel like a fun place to work. I actually started a decorative file folder club. Don't laugh! I picked up colorful files to replace the plain manila ones. I even mailed extras to friends and clients, telling them why I was doing it. Now they had decorative file folders to hold their unpleasant bills, never-ending to-do lists, etc. Not only did they use them and smile at their beauty, but they also thought of me every time they looked at them. My mother-in-law taught me that when choosing something to live with, we should *make it pretty*. Why not place pretty pillows around your office? Why not have pretty dresses in your closet? Why not treat yourself to a spa day or a craft day? Why not plant flowers and surround yourself with loving animals?

Another strategy for creating a healthy environment is to surround yourself with people who will support you. Life is a journey of pop quizzes and finals, and you don't have to take those exams alone. Create a lifeline and *use it*! Although you may not think of them as such, you may already have a personal "board of advisors"—those close friends and family in whom you confide and to whom you look for advice. My brother Ivan is a doctor, so I ask him for medical advice. One of my girlfriends has an objective view of my life, so I trust her opinion and ask her for relationship advice, both personal and professional. I ask an avid gardener acquaintance what to do about my ant problem. I ask a client who has lived in a hurricane area for personal tips on how to deal with hurricanes when I'm in Florida. (And yes, we lived through a recent one.) Do not be afraid to confide in people and ask for help. There is nothing people enjoy more than giving advice, especially when it isn't their lives on the line.

I highly recommend you go one step further and create a professional board of advisors. Because of the industry I am in, mine includes estate lawyers, CPAs, realtors, and mortgage bankers, to name a few. These are all people who can provide services not just for me but also for my clients. A friend who earned his MBA at one of the top business schools told me the most important thing he learned there was knowing when he needed an expert and how to hire and use that expert. I can reach out to my board members for an opinion when new tax legislation has been passed, when I need an interpretation of real estate law, or when I have a client with a low credit score that needs to buy a home. And because I am able to refer my clients to this group of professionals, my clients in turn feel they are wrapped in a cocoon of expertise.

The most important criteria when setting up your board are compatibility and competency, because the board model creates a place for mutually beneficial sharing of referrals, ideas, and information. Most of the gatherings in my industry are simply people I already interface with, and I want a board that's composed of people outside my circle. Of course, I expect these advisors to show up when my clients need them. I cannot have my clients complaining to me that a referred CPA has not returned their calls or that a referred realtor decided to leave town for a month after listing their house.

Having a professional board works best if you can set it up as a two-way street. In my case, my advisors help me by helping my clients or sending referrals to me; I help them by sending my clients to them and also by offering my research and financial expertise. I also support them in other, less tangible ways: I remember their important life anniversaries. I send fresh fruit during tax season. I offer my advice pro bono to every client they send my way. In the early years, I met weekly with my professional board for breakfast, but over the years, as people have retired, moved away, or changed professions, we've begun to hold more meetings by phone, email, or text. However, I do believe that if you are just starting out, it's critical to meet with your board in person to cultivate your relationships with these important advisors.

As an example of another board, a realtor would not only need my expertise on ascertaining whether their clients can afford a second home or what to do with the proceeds of a house sale. They would also need a title company, a mortgage consultant, a home inspector, a construction company, and an interior designer on their professional board of advisors. Who should be on your board?

Learn to Be Yourself

One of the things it took me a long time to learn was that trying to fit in should not be a woman's goal in a male-dominated office. I'm thankful that Strip-O-Grams went out in the 1990s; before then, every guy in the office celebrated his birthday with a stripper performing in the conference room. And women like me weren't just exposed to this objectification of women on special occasions. I once had a colleague who married one of those strippers and would take us out for lunch to watch her at a nearby strip club. I was young (not yet thirty) and wanted to fit in. So I went along with the guys and told some off-color jokes. I was too young to know it was a disaster waiting to happen. I was reported to HR for making inappropriate sexual comments. They got *me* before I got *them*. What was I thinking? Even today, while you don't have to take trying to fit in to the extreme, as I did in those days, a woman must still play the game to an extent if she is to be accepted in a male-dominated office. Let me give you some hard-earned words of advice for women on how to play that game:

Do not dress overly sexually, or you will not be taken seriously.

And dress according to what is appropriate in your field. I'm in a corporate world where money is taken seriously, so I must dress seriously. Neutrality is the best option; black pants and a colorful shirt have been my mainstay since I stepped out of suits. If you are in the fashion industry or interior design, though, by all means dress boldly and fashionably; it's expected there.

Choose your words carefully.

Avoid giggling, and eliminate unnecessary interjections such as *um*, *like*, and *I don't know*. Also, try speaking in a lower voice that is commanding, and enunciate to be heard. This will help you portray the person you want to be. Never hesitate to show you are intelligent, have good ideas and suggestions worthy of sharing, and deserve a spot at the table.

Present yourself with poise.

I have taught women how to shake a hand, walk, and even eat. I have my interns and assistants shadow me so I can model the behavior I expect from them. I take them to meetings. I let them listen in on my phone calls and read my emails so they can emulate my writing style. Since I can't show you how to do this in a book, I encourage you to ask a friend that you respect how to do these things, or search on YouTube for some how-to lessons.

Demand respect.

While I've reached an age where I simply don't care what others think, I must admit I remain aware. Getting respect is really a matter of giving respect. I don't want to intimidate my coworkers or clients, but I do want them to respect me. And, since I expect and demand respect from them, I'm careful not to give them ammunition to belittle me behind my back.

Be a professional.

If you want to be treated as a professional, become a professional. That may require taking courses on your own time, pursuing training opportunities within or outside your company, and subscribing to newsletters, blogs, or podcasts that are related to your industry. Stay current with events and issues, not just relating to your industry but to world events as well. And create and maintain an active network of industry and personal contacts, including the board of advisors discussed earlier. If you see yourself as a professional, act as a professional, and do your job as a professional—whatever that job may be—others will see you that way too.

Do the Opposite

I have worked for at least forty male managers throughout my career. Each left their own particular sear on my psyche, but there was one uniform lesson I learned from all of them: do the opposite of what they were doing. James Madison wrote early drafts of the United States Constitution while isolated in a small room of a home located in the Virginia countryside. How did he craft such a masterpiece? He ordered four hundred books and had them shipped from Europe. He studied how all the great civilizations had been governed—and how they had died. Once he understood what had caused failures in the past, he wrote our constitution to ensure the new government would do exactly the opposite.

In the early years, one of my managers threw notepads at my ass to get my attention. Another liked to tap ashes from his cigar over my desk, and yet another took a simple client email and escalated it to a complaint so I would have a legal mark on my record when I quit his office. One manager told me he had installed face-recognition software in the office and in the parking lot so he could watch my every move; another accused me of harassing his wife at a party when in fact *he* was facing a class-action lawsuit for female harassment. The examples of how I was treated differently from how men were treated could go on and on. I was assigned an outside parking spot in 110-degree weather while the guys were given covered, inside parking. And male colleagues were often given hiring contracts with easy goals, so they could meet their bonuses, while I struggled to meet impossible metrics written into my contracts.

I have had far too many male managers who got high on power. Sometimes they acted like my friends before they were promoted; then they turned on me and made my life miserable with their newfound power. One trader threw his W-2 down onto the desk in front of me every time we had a discussion—I guess to show me who earned the most money and therefore was more important. I even had managers tell me I did not deserve any office space whatsoever. And then there were the managers who brought their sons into the office to be second-in-command, even though I was more deserving. Nepotism in offices is such a disheartening, but common, occurrence in my industry—and I assume many others. I've also had managers insist I convert to Judaism, or Christianity, or become a Mormon—whatever *they* believed would help me do my job better and make them more money. Many of the men I worked for, and with, simply had no idea how to talk to me, so they just didn't. In those early days, before I learned to speak up, I met every situation the same—with silence—in an attempt not to say the wrong thing. So many managers, causing so much distress!

And then there was all the sex: married managers having affairs with my assistants and others having sex with interns in the stairwell or in the parking lot. It was plain debauchery, right in my face. Some guys would actually hire strippers as assistants and then fight over the chattel.

In addition to the ways the men mistreated me—and other women—I saw countless instances where they misbehaved in other ways as the stress of the job wore them down, which became a major lesson for me to do the opposite. I remember one guy ripping the phone out of his wall and throwing it against his glass door—who knew why? Others got drunk or high on drugs in the office. And some were just simply unstable; in fact, suicides among my male colleagues were rampant. One manager shot himself because he was demoted. Another hung himself in his garage after a dispute with his boss. One committed suicide at a firing range, and another gassed himself with balloon helium to avoid facing prosecution.

What did I do when I became a manager? I chose to do the opposite to avoid this mayhem. I treated people with respect. I did not allow drugs or debauchery in the office. And I became a good listener, making it easy for those working for me to vent their frustrations.

While I did not automatically give them what they wanted, I was liberal in giving them time off to deal with personal issues, and I was very straightforward about what I would and wouldn't do about office and work issues. Most importantly, I followed through on any actions I had promised and kept them informed of the outcome. Most of the time, the simple act of letting them know they had been heard was enough. Little did I realize being a successful manager only meant I now had to deal with the same BS from the guys above me on the regional management platform. To this day, there isn't a single manager from my past, at any level, whom I would call to spend time chatting about the *good old days*.

Accept Your Failures

Let me end this chapter by talking about the importance of being able to accept and move on from failure. One of the most fundamental lessons I have learned about self-acceptance is the need to be brutally honest with yourself. For me, that meant acknowledging when my current trajectory was veering off course—especially when I found myself leaning toward the behaviors or stress indicators all those men exhibited. I learned to force myself to stay on the opposite course and make appropriate adjustments. It's hard to make a change, and it's even harder to admit failure. The fact is this: I have failed numerous times, personally as well as professionally. I have made mistakes in hiring. I have made mistakes taking on clients with whom I knew I would struggle to relate. I have said things to friends that I regret saying. Again, that's life! The one thing I have never done is violate my clients' and friends' trust when they share with me their innermost secrets and concerns.

The point here is that I did not let my failures, mistakes, setbacks, or things out of my control stop me—and you must not let those sorts of challenges stop you either. Never be afraid of change, nor of failure. As Verghese recommended at the beginning of this chapter, own your own slippers. Slippers are all about comfort, so when we own our slippers, we must be comfortable with who we are and where we walk.

CHAPTER FIVE

LOVE WHAT YOU DO

If you talk about it, it's a dream, if you envision it, it's possible, but if you schedule it, it's real.

—Tony Robbins, *Get the Edge*

t's as simple as this; love what you do or find another job. Or let me quote Mark Twain: "Find a job you enjoy doing, and you will never have to work a day in your life."

Find and Follow Your Passion

I understand that most young people have no idea what they want to do or what career path to take. Many of my clients who are parents ask me to speak to their children to give them career advice. I first recommend they read *What Color Is Your Parachute? A Practical Manual for Job-Hunters and Career-Changers* by Richard N. Bolles. With ten million copies sold in twenty-eight countries, this is the world's most popular book to guide people in choosing a career. Of course, I also advise them to take advantage of the skill and aptitude tests available at high schools and colleges, on the internet, and on phone apps that cover the same subject. All these tools explore who you are as a person and what you want out of life, whether you are a young adult graduating from high school or college or whether you are facing a midlife crisis. These tests attempt to match your interests with your skills to figure out appropriate and compatible career paths. I find it interesting that young people and women seem open to getting help in making these types of life-changing decisions, while older men drag their feet.

One of the best pieces of advice I can give young people is to reach out to adults they know or admire. There is no one, and I mean *no one*, who—when asked by a truly interested person to speak for a few minutes about their life, their career, and how they got there—will say *no*. People love to talk about themselves! It's sad how rarely others ask, because so many people have insights, advice, and admonishments about the question *What should I do with my life?* Everyone has successes, failures, and regrets. "If I had to do it all over again" is a common human game. All you're doing is asking them to reflect on that thought out loud to you. In addition to being happy to do it, they will be honored you asked. Personally, I love to talk about my life and my career. One of the reasons I have taken the time to write this book is because I believe it will help others.

A truly powerful learning tool when planning a career is shadowing someone for a few days. I arrange for everyone on my staff to shadow different divisions within my company to ensure they like the division they are in. This process is like trying on shoes. Do you prefer sales or operations? Does this career opportunity fit right? Do you like walking in these shoes? Several of my employees have chosen to change departments after this experience. And those who stayed? They saw how the business machine operates and walked away enlightened. They now understand how the various departments work, communicate, and are interconnected. They have seen where the bottlenecks might be, and they understand more fully how to keep the machine operating smoothly.

My business—and quite frankly, my passion—is money. Money has been my focus since I started in the industry when I was eighteen. Unlike many, if not most, of my male colleagues, who are in the industry because they came from families with money, I started because I *needed* money to continue studying at USC. Dealing with money not only became my vocation; it became my avocation. I love it. I love every aspect of it. I control my own career, and I influence other people's lives for the better.

Love Your Career

One of my clients, Rebecca, was a highly successful Hollywood lawyer. She literally ran Hollywood television production through actor and studio contract negotiations representing all the top names. However, Rebecca was anything but successful when it came to running her family's financial or other affairs. She was a four-foot-two Italian ball of fire entirely focused on, and devoted to, her business. She did not have the time or inclination to take care of the needs of her adopted children or the grandchildren she ultimately had to raise. I came into Rebecca's life over two decades ago to help her with money management and estate planning. But our relationship quickly evolved into one where I sometimes even took her place in family matters and also became her trusted confidant and advisor in her complicated occupation. Yet, the hardest was still to come.

Over the years, we proudly watched her children graduate but were then disappointed in their failed marriages. We became dismayed over their drug dependencies and shocked at their suicide attempts. It was a never-ending drama of family issues that, as the family matriarch, fell on Rebecca's shoulders and ultimately on me. Together, we made it through it all—until recently. This past year Rebecca was diagnosed with full dementia and now requires twenty-four-seven assistance. I'm still here to schedule the home health care providers and assist her husband through these dismal years of incontinence and memory loss. And so much loss: The loss of a vibrant life. The loss of one of the brightest minds in Hollywood. The loss of a matriarch—the matriarch of a disintegrating family. We are losing an amazing woman, and as hard as dealing with her deteriorating health has been, getting to know and being a part of Rebecca's and other extraordinary people's lives has been what I have loved most about the career I have chosen.

I'm still helping manage Rebecca's financial affairs. Over the years we built a level of trust, and with her approval and confidence in me, we set up trusts as part of the estate planning process. These trusts will support the family for the next two generations. As the named trustees, my firm and I ensure that she, her husband, and her beneficiaries will always be cared for.

Why am I telling you all this? I want to give you an example of how a career involving your passion—in my case, money—can also be one you love. For me, I find joy when I am able to influence so many other people's lives for the better. I also want to show you why I do what I do and why I've been willing to put up with all the trials and tribulations women in my industry are forced to endure. My client-advisor relationship with Rebecca became a wonderful friendship that will never leave my heart. It's because of these interpersonal relationships that I've been willing to put up with all the industry and office abuse over all these years. And it's also why it's so important that I love my clients—at least most of the time. When you love someone as I grew to love Rebecca, you will overcome any obstacles thrown in your path. Knowing that my clients and I will be able to handle life's trials together makes my choice of a career that requires me to get up at dawn, just to face one issue after another, all worthwhile. It's been forty years—forty years full of clients who have become and remain my family!

Stay Focused on Your Passion

Financial planning and managing money can be a natural career fit for women. We are trustworthy, detail orientated, and risk-averse with clients' monies. There are numerous studies that show women's performance in managing portfolios is as good as, or even better than, that of men. So why is there such a low participation rate of women in our industry? I think the answer is clear: women must also endure the abuse and sexism in a male-dominated environment.

From another viewpoint, you see very few women, but not an insignificant number of men, being sent to prison for misdeeds in my industry. Unfortunately, the name of the game has historically been *he who makes the most money wins*, and too many men will do whatever it takes to win. I sometimes wonder if the reason women don't stay in this business is because they have no desire to be ruthless or dishonest. I also wonder what the passions really are for the men who come into this field. I know my passion is to make the lives of my clients better. However, it has been my observation that the passion of most men is more focused on making money than it is serving the needs of their clients. If that is true, I doubt they ever truly loved their careers as I do.

I cannot tell you how often I have sat with a new or prospective client and, in our discussions, been told, "All I hear from my current money manager is *no*." When I ask them what they want to do with their lives and they say they want to travel, buy a vacation home, help a relative, or something similar, it's often clear they have enough assets to do what they want. Sadly, the reason their current financial planner told them no is often one of two reasons: He just wants to focus on making money and does not want to put in the time it takes to get to know his clients and actively manage their accounts to meet their wants, as well as their needs. Or, and I believe this is all too common, his bonuses are based upon how much money he keeps under management; therefore, he wants to keep their funds in their account as long as possible. By keeping the client scared about whether they will have enough money in retirement, and simply saying no to their withdrawal requests, he accomplishes his personal objective. Recently, a new client put it very succinctly: "You mean I can actually spend some of my money *now*? I don't have to save it all for retirement?"

Whether working as a financial advisor or in other fields, too often people get caught up in just getting by, and they lose sight of their true passions. They stop loving their jobs, if they ever did, and become motivated by other forces—often money. If you let money be the primary driver in your life, you can be held hostage by it. I view money differently. I see money as freedom: the freedom to do what you want. I work with my clients to achieve their desires and enjoy what their money can provide them. Together, we outline their dreams, develop their plans to make their dreams come true, and then budget and schedule out the steps to get where they want to go. By staying true to my passion for helping other people achieve their goals, I have been able to love my job over the course of four decades, even when the going got tough.

CHAPTER SIX

SURVIVE AND FLOURISH

The question isn't who is going to let me; it's who is going to stop me.

—paraphrased from *The Fountainhead*,
by Ayn Rand

hope my story about how I survived in a male-dominated business can help every woman in a similar situation, whether she's in finance, engineering, high technology, construction, manufacturing, the auto industry, a business start-up—any other area where men tend to dominate. The most important thing I can tell you is that if you love the challenge of what you are doing, you must stick with it. If you don't—if you quit trying and let others win—you will have regrets. That said, I know few of us are cut out to endure the day-to-day battles and suffer the bruises and scars along the way. Let me share some of the lessons I have learned that have helped me not just survive but flourish.

Avoid Sexual Misunderstandings and Advances

This is a topic so central to interactions between men and women that I have addressed it before and will again. Men often mistake a woman's friendship and kindness for a desire of intimacy; they just can't get past the sex. As I mentioned in Chapter 4, it's important to dress so that you avoid sexual misunderstanding. Aim for a look that is commanding and deserving of respect, not one suggesting you are sexually available. This is especially important when meeting men for the first time—or even when you have to walk in dark parking lots. It has been proven that people with malicious intent look for vulnerable females in dark areas. But even in safe spaces, it's important to dress appropriately and walk with an air of professional distance so no one mistakes you for someone to be trifled with.

When I participate in group activities outside the office, like corporate trips that entail playing softball, going down river rapids, or interacting at endless cocktail parties and meetings at golf resorts, I likewise take care to not cross the sexual line with what I wear and how I carry myself. I also remind myself, over and over at these sorts of events, that most sexist things said or done by men are usually not done to be malicious; they are simply done out of ignorance. When I believe that is the case, I do not hesitate to confront them, but I do it in a respectful manner rather than in a mean or demeaning way.

Recently, a supervisory colleague exclaimed, "I forget you're a woman! I hope you're not offended!" What he did not realize was that this is precisely my goal with corporate colleagues. I don't want to be seen as a woman in the work environment but rather as an equitable partner. With clients, both men and women, my goal is to have them involuntarily exclaim, "Nora, I love you!" When they do that, I know I have a committed client who will be in my life for a very long time.

Learn to Read the Room

When you walk into a room, whether it's a one-on-one meeting, a conference room, or a business cocktail party, start out being quiet and observant. Learn to read the room, understand what is happening, and see how the game is being played. Once you identify the agenda and people's motivations, decide what your role should be: Are you a subordinate and expected to remain quiet, or are you a leader and expected to lead and talk? Then listen or talk according to the rules of the room. It's really that simple.

I cannot stress enough how important it is to learn how to listen more than talk. Are you anxious about a client meeting? Petrified at corporate gatherings? If so, then don't talk. Let the others do the talking. People love hearing their own voices, and they will remember you as that fabulous, very bright person who *listened*. For the most part, my clients and coworkers know little about my hobbies or my passions. They don't know my political or religious beliefs. They don't even know what I like to eat or the sports I love. And you know what? They probably don't care. Customers, clients, and coworkers want you to be happy and to have a full and varied life, but they don't really want to hear the details unless they are in charge of office gossip—and in that case, you want to avoid them at all costs. What most people want is to be heard and to tell you about themselves. So stop talking and become an exceptional listener. You will be amazed what you learn and how you can use it to your benefit.

When you do decide to contribute to the conversation, make sure your words are positive and uplifting. Talk about your successes. No one wants to hear that their financial advisor, who's in charge of handling their entire family's wealth, is depressed or that she recently and royally screwed up a real estate purchase. This is not just good advice for financial planners; it applies to everyone working in a professional capacity. How much do you know about the personal life of your doctor, your dentist, or your attorney? Keep it that way with your own personal life. Otherwise, a competitor may discover your weak spots and exploit them. How do I know? Because that's exactly what I do. As I mentioned earlier, I keep a dossier on my competition and other key people with whom I interact. I would advise you to do the same. Don't just keep track of their flaws; keep a record of all the positives about the key people in your life, including your competitors: their hobbies, their priorities, and their families. This data will help you be an engaging conversationalist at meetings and conferences and will also help you focus on discussion points that are important to them.

The other thing to keep in mind when working the room is to take advantage of your talents. You have developed your own skills and expertise; why not use them? As discussed in Chapter 4, being a professional means taking courses, subscribing to journals, and otherwise staying current with events and issues within your industry and throughout the world. There is nothing worse than not having an informed opinion or being able to discuss important issues and current events at business functions.

Learn to Delegate

It has been my experience that women are, by nature, insecure about delegating work to others. It's outside our comfort zone. But by being totally honest with yourself, and truly knowing your own strengths and weaknesses, along with those of your team, you can learn to delegate with confidence. While you certainly need to assess what you are delegating and to whom, know that delegating does not mean giving up control. I keep close tabs on whomever I am delegating to until I feel comfortable that the probation period is over. Once I can trust them to complete a task as I would, at my standard of excellence, I leave them alone. Even then, delegating involves reporting, follow-up, and monitoring. Delegating is a way of managing that allows you to focus on matters that cannot be assigned to someone else. It's also a powerful way to train and retain your team. My experience has been that people who feel they have real responsibility and who are given the authority and freedom to carry out their responsibilities are better and more loyal team members. Once you are comfortable that the right reporting and control mechanisms are in place, delegating becomes a powerful tool to free your time and expand your business.

Know Your Strengths

As someone charged with dealing with clients and managing their money, my strengths include:

1. Being a good listener and getting people comfortable confiding in me by never being negative or judgmental.
2. Knowing how to overcome objections.
3. Skillfully conversing with people in person, over the telephone, on texts, or by email.
4. Developing workable, real-life strategies for almost any situation with which I am faced.
5. Admitting when I'm wrong and quickly changing direction as circumstances dictate.
6. Showing up on time, and meeting or exceeding commitments to deliver what I have promised.
7. And last, but not least, knowing what I do not know, and knowing when I need the assistance of a professional expert.

One of the issues I deal with daily, specific to my profession, is knowing when to pull the trigger to buy and sell investments. I deal with this by having strict buy and sell strategies, which I have developed over the years. It's called experience. Conversely, many in my industry fail due to *paralysis by analysis*, meaning they cannot quickly make timely investment-related decisions. As for picking specific individual stocks, I learned long ago that I'm not an analyst. If I loved spreadsheets, I would have completed an MBA and become an analyst myself, but I did not. And, while my record has proven that I'm an excellent portfolio manager, I've learned to listen to certain analysts whose judgment I have come to trust and whose entire focus and profession is picking stocks. The bottom line is this: know your strengths, make a list like I did above, and focus on them. But also know when you need the assistance of a professional expert, and don't hesitate to seek them out and listen to their advice.

Get Yourself Promoted

No one will promote you if you just sit there and hope that some upper-echelon man sees your outstanding work product. If you just sit quietly and don't speak up, why would anyone promote you and pay you a higher salary when they can get that outstanding work product at a lower cost? Learn from men. They ask for, even demand, jobs for which they have absolutely no experience. While I am not telling you to demand a job for which you have no experience, I am telling you to be aggressive in pursuing the job or promotion you believe you deserve. Let me tell you how.

It starts by visualizing your dream job. If it exists where you currently work, discuss career options with a manager or someone within the company whom you trust, especially if that is a person you want to work with or for. Write down why you would be excellent at doing the job and why you deserve the opportunity, and then don't just walk in and ask for it; walk in and *demand* it, along with a deadline for confirmation of your request. Is this a risk? Yes, but I've found it a risk worth taking. If you get a "No," it's time to re-create yourself, which probably means moving to a competing firm. A truism in business is that it's often necessary to change companies in order to be promoted and paid what you're worth. The very act of visualizing, writing it down, and making a case for yourself will build your confidence. Then you will be ready to walk in with confidence, demand the promotion, set a deadline, and see what happens. Men do it all the time. As a woman, you need to do it too.

Just so you don't think I'm telling you to be brash and arrogant, let me expand on this a little. You've done your homework and your visualization, so you have the confidence part down. Then, when you meet with your manager, be upfront with him and don't make him try to guess why you're there. That is, after any small talk, be blunt yet courteous and positive: "Bill, I'm sure you agree it's time to discuss a promotion." But before you do any demanding, review for him what you have accomplished, why you are deserving of a promotion, how it will help him and the firm, and, if it means a change in position, how your promotion will not leave him shorthanded. Let him know you understand he may need some time, especially if he needs to confer with others, but do not let the conversation end without a specific time for follow-up and a decision. Then, as I said, see what happens.

Become Unstoppable

Let me end the chapter by assuring you that, if you take the advice in this chapter, including learning how to read the room, knowing your strengths, and being willing to take action to promote your career, you will not only survive and flourish, but you will also become *unstoppable*. At that point no one can stop you but yourself.

When asked who my biggest competitor is, I always reply, "Myself." It's up to you to determine how much effort you want to put into your career and what goals you want to reach. It's up to you to know when the path you're taking is veering off course and you need to take another tack. And of course it's up to you to say what you are satisfied with, what fulfills you, and when it's time to say, "*No more—I call the shots for my life—no one else does.*"

Earlier I told the story of the man who blocked the conference room door and threatened to kill us all. That was one of my "no more" times. It's not unusual as I get to know a newly divorced client that she will relate to me how she had reached a "no more" time and had taken action to end her marriage. Similarly, it's not unusual for a friend or client, usually younger, to confide in me that they hate their job and have reached a "no more" time. It is in these situations where I feel most needed, and in fact, it's when I do my best work as we work together to create new goals and plans to execute the changes they are now committed to make. It is at these times that they have become—unstoppable.

CHAPTER SEVEN

MANAGE YOUR CLIENTS AND YOUR TEAM

If your actions create a legacy that inspires others to dream more, learn more, do more, and become more, then, you are an excellent leader.

—Dolly Parton

No matter what your profession or what you do, knowing how to deal with people is a vital skill in achieving success and happiness—not just in business, but in all of life. Let me start by telling you a few of the ways I grow and manage my team and teach them to deal with clients.

Manage with Integrity

A fundamental tenet that successful managers embrace is making decisions with integrity, and that starts with hiring. I look for two key qualities that cannot be taught: ambition and honesty. I look for people who will show up and who have a moral compass, and I avoid those who are driven by anger or greed. There is a huge difference between wanting to make money and being greedy. Greed has no morals, and greedy people have no place on my team.

I also hire assistants who I believe can learn quickly, welcome challenges, and arrive on time, ready to face the day. I can teach the rest. Experience is good, but I find that if I hire a candidate who has worked for years in our industry, she is often stuck in her own ways, disillusioned with her job path, and resistant to change. I prefer a fresh-page hire whom I can influence and motivate to do whatever specific job my team needs. When hiring, that leads me to heavily focus on *personality over experience*. I recommend you do the same. You can change an adult's experience level through training and exposure to new tasks and responsibilities. But rarely can you change an adult's personality. Remember these critical points when hiring, and you will seldom be faced with the painful but sometimes extremely necessary task of firing.

Once you have your team in place, you must *always* have their backs. Never criticize anyone on your team in front of a client. Doing so will not make you look smarter; on the contrary, it will make you look dumb for having hired such an inept person. Always stand up for your team. They will repay you with loyalty and speak up and stand by you when others disparage you or anyone else on your team.

I follow a similar philosophy about integrity when dealing with clients. When it comes to successfully managing their portfolios, I educate clients to the point where they understand what I'm doing and the reasons why. That way I'm able to discuss the actions I'm taking, and clients will not hesitate to question me in an informed way about those actions. Most importantly, I never, ever give clients a reason to question my integrity or on whose side of the table I sit. They know I care about them and their lives. This is apparent not just with my words, but also with my actions.

Communicate Effectively

I teach my team that the key to any conversation starts with listening, as discussed in Chapter 6. You learn nothing new when you are the one doing the talking. And listening means not just hearing a client's words but recognizing the client's tone. Are they angry or simply looking for an answer or clarification?

In my industry, and I'm sure it's the same for everyone who deals with customers, it's common and extremely frustrating when clients call to use me as a dumpster. For me, this means a client will go on and on about everything that's wrong with the markets, their accounts, their tax bills, etc. The way I teach my team to deal with these calls is to question and probe to discover the origin of the complaint. While it could be any one of a hundred different things, in most cases I've found the real issue is business or marital difficulties, family issues, or health concerns that lead directly to market (money) concerns. But listening is only step one. Just as important, before responding, is knowing what you are trying to accomplish and what you want the outcome of the conversation to be. Having dealt with thousands of these calls, I've learned that once you know the real issue, your goal should be to prompt the client to say something positive. Just one positive statement amid their deluge of issues and complaints can change the whole conversation. It is not enough for *you* to make the positive statement; you need to get them to do it. It's amazing what this one technique can do. It redirects their thinking from negative to positive and opens the door for a productive conversation.

I have a client who suffers with OCD. In the past, he would call me and talk endlessly with total negativity. Finally, I called him on it.

"If you want to talk to me, start the conversation with something positive. Tell me about the weather, about your grandchild . . . anything. Then I'll listen to every complaint you have."

It took a while, but he now starts every conversation with something positive, as I requested, and sometimes he goes all out. "I just want to tell you how great you are!" And yes, he still has complaints, but by starting out on a positive note, we can discuss his issues on an equal, productive, and problem-solving basis.

This, of course, does not always work. I call this phenomenon "exceeding the ratio of no's." This occurs when you are full to the brim and cannot stand one more negative comment or one more fight, whether it be with clients, colleagues, supervisors, or team members. I stop, take a break, get a cup of coffee, or go for a walk. Sometimes I just wait another day. And I highly recommend it to everyone. You will be amazed how a night's sleep can resolve issues and allow you to have better communications the next day.

My experience has shown me that most lawsuits are due to a lack of communication. If a client has so frustrated or annoyed you that you are no longer willing to communicate with them in a positive manner, then hand them off to someone who can. My personal litmus test is asking myself, "If I switched firms tomorrow, would I ask this person to go with me?" If the answer is no, then it's time to transfer them to someone who will work with them in a positive manner.

Good communication, therefore, is partly about listening and partly about keeping things positive. And in my business, communication almost always involves dealing with managing complaints and frustrations, and for that I use a four-step process:

1. Listen. Let the other person fully explain their issue.
2. Empathize. Repeat back what they said to reassure them you heard correctly. This can greatly reduce their anxiety.
3. Don't be defensive. If you were wrong, take responsibility and admit it.
4. If possible, give a solution. If that's not possible, give them a precise time when you will follow up, and then follow up *before* that time, even if you are simply telling them you need more time to resolve their issue.

Train and Support Your Team

How you train, support, and manage your team can make or break your chances for success. To start, make sure everyone understands and is fully committed to achieving the goals you have set for your team. When it comes to giving specific instructions, make sure those instructions and the outcome you expect are clearly understood. If it's a complicated task, ask if there are questions or, better yet, have them repeat your instructions back to you. That way you will know for sure they heard and understand what is expected. I cannot believe how many people just bark out orders, walk away, and then are disappointed when a task is not completed to their liking. If at all possible, explain not just what you want done, but why it is important that it be done. For example, if you say you want a certain Excel spreadsheet on some data, you will want your team member to know *why*. It will make them feel part of the process, and it will also help develop their skills and knowledge about how your business flows and functions.

Other tips to train and manage a team include:

Create an environment where your team members have an open and free forum to give you feedback.

This is accomplished not just by telling them that you want their feedback but also by ensuring that anything they have to say is acknowledged and discussed. To get started with a new team, this may require setting a specific time for review and feedback and a specific forum for this exchange. But once members realize you are truly open to hearing what they have to say, the feedback will flow.

Take your team members with you to meetings—or everywhere.

As discussed in an earlier chapter, they learn by seeing you in action. They need to observe your body language, listen to the inflection of your voice, understand how you interact with others, and watch how you overcome objections.

When you bring them along, you can also show them how to travel, how to dress, and how to conduct themselves using good business etiquette. It's surprising how few people have been taught these things, either by family or friends.

Find each team member's strengths, and create a job position to draw upon those strengths.

One of my assistants is extremely good with elderly clients, so she is our "Client Concierge." The other assistant, who loves analytics and does my meeting prep and analysis work, is our "Analytics Coordinator." Finding out what makes your team members happy is also helpful. Get to know who they are and how they visualize *their* perfect day; then match their workday to that vision. Don't put an introvert in a traveling sales position!

Arrange regular retreats.

I do one quarterly, outside the office, to allow team members to get to know each other on a more personal level. We talk about ourselves and not about work. You can set up a book club with discussions. Arrange an amusing karaoke session in the privacy of your home. Plan arts and crafts to encourage each of them to connect with their inner child. Or take them to an elegant restaurant where they need to get dressed up and act differently than they normally do. These retreats can be as easy as an excursion to a nearby day spa after work or a fun lunch for the team at a local ramen bar or dim sum restaurant. The point is to arrange different activities that are out of our daily rituals where we can talk about ourselves rather than work or client matters.

Surprise your team with small gifts.

It lets them know you are thinking of them on your business trips and on weekends. These don't have to be expensive gifts; I'm talking about an exotic seashell from a client's beach wedding, a funny magnet from a curio shop, or a book from a museum you visited. These are just a few examples.

Overpay your staff.

That's right—I have always overpaid everyone working for me. Why? The paychecks you give your staff are essential to ensure their loyalty and inspire them to work to the level for which they are being paid. With higher pay, they will work harder and ensure their performance is worthy of their income; meanwhile, you will receive more productivity and tenfold less complaining.

Enact the following rule: *no complaints unless you want a solution from me.*

For decades, I've been in an industry that is highly regulated, requiring endless documentation, forms, and processes. I hate hearing complaints about issues that have nothing to do with me or over which I have no control. I tell my team that I'm not in charge of the SEC (Securities and Exchange Commission), and I don't want to hear complaints about their rules and regulations that I have no power to change. "Stop the negativity!" I tell them. "Offer solutions to the powers that be, not to me." If I don't have the authority to resolve these issues, then I don't want grievances left at my door. For my own part, I practice what I preach and am constantly sending emails to others with suggestions about how they can help me do my job better or more easily.

Offer educational opportunities.

And genuinely care about your staff's future. The better their resumes, the better their career paths will be. Do not be afraid to lose team members to greater opportunities; instead, be afraid they will dislike you for holding them back. I had an assistant who never attended college, but with my support and insistence, she took advantage of our corporate school reimbursement policy and ended up with an associate degree. Her smile at graduation was my present.

Get to know the important people in your team members' lives.

While it may not be easy or even possible to actually meet their family and friends, make sure it's easy for team members to talk and share stories about them with you. It's all part of being a good listener and being truly interested in them as people. Besides your significant other, your team members are your premier clients. Treat them as such. If you are kinder, more empathetic, and more patient with a client or your life partner than you are with your team members, then you had better check your priorities. If you don't make yelling at your spouse a habit, why would you yell at your assistants?

Be flexible with their hours.

Children get sick, loved ones die, pets need to go to the vet. Give those who work for you time to heal when necessary, and nurture them by letting them know they need not worry or feel guilty for taking time off from work. Resist the temptation to text or email them while they are dealing with personal problems. Make sure, if the situation is dire, that you plan for their personal time off by delegating their duties to others. Let your people turn their full attention to dealing with their personal crises.

Give your team members space in the evenings and during the weekends.

You want them coming to work refreshed and reinvigorated after time off. Again, that means not texting or sending emails or otherwise interrupting them when they are away from the office. If you are diligent about giving them this time uninterrupted, when the rare occasion arises when you truly need them to stay late or work over a weekend, they will know that what needs to be done is truly important, and they will respond positively, rather than with an *oh, not again* attitude. Also, on a Friday afternoon, never tell them ominously, "I have something to discuss with you on Monday," as this will surely ruin their weekend. Be kind. Let your staff have these off hours to themselves. And although I encourage getting to know everyone on your team, it's also critical to respect their privacy. You don't need to know what they did during the weekend or while they were on personal leave. If they want to share that information, they'll tell you.

Protect your team members from bullies.

Stand up for them against troublemakers in your office as well as difficult clients. If my assistant is having a bad day, I'm going to have a bad day. Loyalty is a two-way street, but you must show your loyalty first. A few years ago, a senior male portfolio manager was mad at his assistant over some perceived error. Unfortunately, *my* assistant was the only person around to bear the brunt of his frustration. I was inside my office when I heard a commotion. As I opened my office door, I heard only the tail end of a tirade as he leaned over her desk, berating her, before turning and stomping away. She didn't work for him; she just happened to be the nearest punching bag. I could not stand for this—not only because her day had been ruined, but because now mine would be as well. In this case, I called her into my office, told her how wrong his actions were, and assured her I would talk with him to ensure it never happened again. But, unless she felt it needed to be done immediately, I told her I thought it best to wait until the end of the day and do it after work in a less confrontational setting. She agreed. After most people had left for the day, I went into his office and sat down, and before he could even ask why I was there, he calmly admitted how wrong his actions were. As is so often the case, his anger had died down and he was readily reticent. While I decided not to push him to the point of demanding an apology or referring him to HR, I did make it clear that I would not tolerate a repeat of his actions. The next day, I told my assistant the action I had taken, and to his credit he did stop by and apologize to her for what he had done. When you think about how critical your team is to your own success and happiness, remember whatever you hated about your own job when you were a team member and—as I mentioned earlier—*do the opposite*.

Respond with Common Courtesy

Over the years, I've been responsible for numerous trainees. The primary thing I teach is remarkably simple. The universe will reward you endlessly if you do just two small things: *show up on time and return phone calls*. Today, a "phone call" can be more than what it once was: it can be a text, an email, or a message on Facebook, LinkedIn, Instagram, or myriad other social media platforms. I teach my team that whichever method our client chooses to communicate with, we need to communicate back by the same method and in the same language. Clients who email requests don't want a phone call. And if a client texts you, they are not looking for a phone call or a letter. It's not difficult; it's just common sense and common courtesy.

I'm constantly surprised how difficult it seems for 99 percent of the population to do this remarkably simple thing and do it in a timely manner. Try calling, emailing, or texting the following people: your doctor, your CPA, your cable company, your plumber, or your computer tech, with the expectation of getting a timely response. I have taught my team to return every communication as quickly as possible, but in no case should they wait longer than twenty-four hours to respond and forty-eight hours to resolve issues. If that is not possible, they are trained to communicate the reason why and establish a time schedule that's acceptable to the client, with a commitment to keep the client updated on progress. Then my team knows they must meet or exceed what they have promised.

Develop Realistic Expectations

I teach my team to do everything in their power to see that reality exceeds expectations. I have mentioned the importance of promptly responding to client communications. Let me tell you why. It all has to do with expectations and reality. If you promise to return a call in an hour and you return it in two, the client sees you as wasting their time. And you lose. But if you tell them you will return the call in three hours and you do it in two, the client sees you as being professional and efficient. And you win. Think about it. It's a simple concept!

This concept of reality exceeding expectations does not apply just to returning calls. It applies to most things in life. For example, it's extremely easy to promise a potential client fantastic returns in order to obtain their business. The problem is that, when reality does not meet expectations, you have an unhappy client. So it's a balancing act, and I've found nothing works better than the truth. When faced with an unhappy or concerned client, nothing is *easier* than to tell them what they want to hear and make promises that can't be met. But all you have done is made the issue worse. The truth, upfront, is always the best response. And be very careful that what you consider to be the truth, at that moment, is not just a false rationalization to get out of an uncomfortable call or unseemly situation. Having the personal discipline and a well-trained team that can deliver on what is promised makes for a smoothly run office.

Manage Inevitable Problems

There are times, even when you think you have done everything right, when it becomes clear you made the wrong hiring decision. When that happens, don't hesitate to fire someone. It will be in the best interests of everyone, including the person being fired. When this happens to me, and it has, I often choose to counsel them on their strengths and why those strengths would be better suited in another position. If possible, I give them the opportunity to explore other positions within the company. And I always encourage them to make a pro and con list about their skills and goals. As you know, it's a strategy I use for most difficult decisions, like the time Robby and I were evaluating whether or not to move to Las Vegas. I tell them that by the time their list is completed, they will clearly see they will be happier in another job. By mapping it out, the answer reveals itself.

For me, there are few things I do that are more difficult than firing someone. Before ending this chapter, let me give a quick anecdote that may help you. Early in my career, I was faced with doing my first firing. I tossed and turned at night and spent several days running through my mind exactly what I was going to say. When I finally sat with the person, I had barely gotten started when she looked at me and said, "Nora, don't feel so bad. I know this isn't working out for either of us." What did I learn from this experience? I learned that in the few instances where I've needed to fire someone, they already knew it was a wrong fit. This has allowed me to rationalize that firing someone is not just what I need to do for the good of my business and the other team members, but it's also the right thing to do for them. That way they are free to find a job that fits them, and their skill set, better.

CHAPTER EIGHT

AVOID REGRETS AND FACE YOUR FEARS

We all make mistakes, have struggles, and even regret things in our past. But you are not your mistakes, you are not your struggles, and you are here NOW with the power to shape your day and your future.

—Steve Maraboli, *Unapologetically You: Reflections on Life and the Human Experience*

L iving with regrets and looking backward are human traits that only divert energy to circumstances you cannot change. I speak from experience; in helping clients, even those in their nineties, I deal with their regrets all day long. It never stops.

Let Go

There is an unlimited number of things you should rarely dwell on, like what happened in the past, or the poor choices you've made, or the unshakable feeling that the world is out of your control. I should have bought Microsoft stock ten years ago. If only I had bought that beach property in 1992. I should never have thrown away my childhood toys. It's common to hear someone say, "I would have, I could have, or I should have."

Regrets are stumbling blocks in living; I hear these ruminations every day. Even when people know they cannot change the past, they still find it difficult to look forward. I don't want to hear about winning stocks from twenty years ago; tell me what stocks to invest in for the *next* decade. Don't dwell on or tell me how much you regret your last marriage; tell me your plan for the rest of your life.

In 2001 Robby and I started a company named Ride Home, LLC. Its purpose was to provide pre-paid cab rides so teenagers could get out of troublesome situations without needing to call their parents. Information was stored on a military-type dog tag necklace, and parents could deposit money toward cab rides with no questions asked. As with many small businesses, it was the marketing budget that forced us to close. It was a great idea, but at that time we simply did not have the capital to sustain it. As you can imagine, when Uber was founded in 2009, we looked back and knew we had been on the right path. But we don't live with regrets. We were proud to see that we had an idea whose time had finally come, and hopefully we helped some teenagers in the short time that Ride Home was in business.

I'm writing this paragraph during my very last read-through before sending this book off to the publisher. As I'm doing this final reading, I realize that, by passing on the positive lessons I have learned, I can finally listen to my own advice and *let go* of all the trials, tribulations, harassments, times I was ignored, and belittlements I've endured as a woman struggling for success in a male-dominated industry. By writing this book I can now *let go* of the negative load I've been dragging behind me all these years! What a wonderful feeling to follow my own advice.

Look to the Future, Love Who You Are, and Avoid Jealousy

Mistakes and setbacks are a fact of life. They are how we learn and redirect our path. Also, human beings are ever evolving, each with different needs. What we needed in our twenties is far different from what we need in our sixties. As I wrote in the last section, rather than looking back and dwelling on what could have been, count your blessings and be grateful for what you have accomplished and what you now have. Do this and you will find yourself a much happier and more successful person.

Do you compare yourself to the top producer in your office or workplace and find yourself lacking? Isn't it better to view your success based on achieving your own goals? Do you look at a friend's life and wish it was yours? If there's one thing I've learned about jealousy and coveting your neighbor, it's that you never know what demons they live with. We all have our individual regrets and longings, but we also all have our own demons that possess us.

Be kind to yourself. When you stumble, give yourself a break and the time to recover and learn from the mistake so you don't make it again. Always yearn to be moving forward. One of the keys to a happy life is to look ahead and create a world that will be better tomorrow than it was yesterday. For me that includes a plan to reach both professional goals and personal goals. Make it the same for you. If you think the word *plan* has shown up frequently in this book, you are absolutely right, and you're not done seeing it. Planning is all about the future, and nothing keeps you looking ahead with a positive attitude more than having a plan.

Most of the time, none of this planning requires much money. For example, I wanted to swim more this year, so I not only took advantage of the access to public pools, but I also snorkeled in the ocean. I wanted to read more, so I changed my routine to go to bed earlier, which gave me two hours of uninterrupted reading time. I wanted to expand my professional team, so I interviewed and hired a woman to be my partner and hired an assistant. I wanted to spend more time with friends, so I put in the effort to do it. And there's another thing to think about when learning from your past and planning for your future: relationships are two-way streets. You must put the same time and energy into them that you want to receive in return. It's not easy, and it doesn't just happen. It must be thought about and decided upon; then an action plan must be made and implemented. It's your life; be in control of it.

I grew up within a culture of negativity, and that can fuel fears about the future. I'm sure many of you had that experience as well. We all have little voices in our minds that tell us we're not good enough, smart enough, or popular enough. For me, it was sometimes the voice of my middle brother telling me I had a big butt, and sometimes it was my mother's voice telling me I wasn't as smart as my older brother. It may have been the voice of a boyfriend telling me I wasn't good enough for him or the voice of a friend telling me I was uncaring. Maybe it was the voice of my manager telling me that I should be fired. All these voices were in my head, and at night, while I slept, they told me over and over that I wasn't good enough. I don't have a magic wand to tell you how to make those voices go away, and I'm sure I didn't handle them well when I was young. But today, on the rare occasions when I hear them, I smile and tell them, "Shut up! I'm Nora Castro, and I love who I am."

Who is there to tell us we are *good human beings*? If you're lucky, it was your parents. If you're luckier still, you have a spouse to say this to you today. But there is only one person who truly needs to tell you that you are a good human being. That person is you.

Face Your Fears

I rarely fear tomorrow. As you now know, one of the roles I fill for my clients is being a "life coach." Hopefully, as you're reading this book, I am filling that role for you too. Above all else, my primary advice is to focus on creating and ensuring you have what I've been referring to as an *authentic life*—the life of your dreams. Of course, because of the industry I'm in, the psychology of money is an important focus of my relationship with clients, so let me also give you another bit of advice I give them: To create your authentic life, money—which provides security and allows options—is a critical consideration. If your financial situation is under control, you will be better able to face whatever fears and challenges come along. Is your primary focus the retirement years? Are you a grandparent whose wish it is to leave a sizable inheritance to your children? Do you want to expand your charitable endeavors? Are you about to purchase a new home? Answering those questions, and having a plan to achieve these things, is the surest way to avoid regrets and not fear tomorrow.

As discussed earlier, I always ensure my clients are prepared for life's curveballs, detours, and roadblocks. Are you getting divorced? Planning a pregnancy? Do you or does someone in your family have stage 4 cancer? John Lennon perhaps put it best when he wrote that "life is what happens to you while you're busy making other plans."

As I've noted, a large part of my practice is focused on single, widowed, or divorced women. Some of them found themselves alone quite suddenly and are filled with regrets and fears. Some regretted having children. Others regretted they had married an abusive spouse and how long they had stayed with him. Still others admitted they hate their parents and feel guilty about their inheritance. And almost all are ashamed of many of the choices they have made over the years. These are secrets that clients share with me because they know they will never go beyond my ears. I do not judge. I do not blame. I listen, and I listen very carefully. Then with great thought and a lifetime of real-world experience, unlike a psychologist or psychiatrist who tries to lead them to find answers for themselves, I offer solutions.

Choose Your Tomorrow

We've all made mistakes in the past; we all have concerns about the future. And we all must face the unexpected. As I said, while these mistakes, concerns, and fears may sound like what people might share with a therapist, it's important that I create an atmosphere where my clients, especially women going through the trauma of a divorce or the death of a spouse, can freely share their situations with me. Why? Because if you are a client, I don't see my role as just providing advice. I'm a trusted companion, traveling along the road beside you on your journey to recover and move on from these inevitable life experiences.

The first step is to help you define your future goals and visualize the life of your dreams. I listen to your fears and regrets and use them as a springboard from which to move forward. They also serve as powerful caution signs for what pitfalls you need to avoid.

Second, we will create a budget, so you'll know where your money is going and be able to prove to yourself that you *can* be financially secure. As you learned earlier, and it's worth repeating—you would be surprised how many people have no idea what they spend their money on until they complete this exercise.

The third step is the hard part—creating a plan and a budget to go from where you are today to that dream life you so deserve. It's at this point where most financial planners do their clients a great injustice. Their advice is almost always to cut back, eliminate expenses, or simply say *no*. That is not my approach. I have learned over the years that trade-offs don't always need to be negative. Let me give you some examples.

If you cut back on going out to eat, you can save for a trip to Italy to learn how to cook. If you reduce the number of hours you spend at work, you can decrease daycare costs and create more time with your children. If you stop spending mindless money on clothes, you can start saving toward the sailboat you always wanted. Life is full of choices; my goal is to help you make them and then fulfill the choices you make.

Living with regret and the fear of tomorrow is human nature—but turning those regrets and fears into future actions, by making new life goals and a plan to achieve them, is a positive way of putting the past behind you. It's a way that allows you to look forward to tomorrow. All you need to do is decide to do it. It's your choice to start today.

CHAPTER NINE

GIVE BACK

Humility is not thinking less of yourself; it is thinking of yourself less.

—Rick Warren, *The Purpose Driven Life: What on Earth Am I Here For?*

From my earliest childhood years, I found that helping those around me was what made me happiest. It was undoubtedly something instilled in me by my parents. It might be something as simple as holding a door open, helping an elderly person with a heavy bag, or picking up a piece of trash. And I have always loved giving gifts. At Christmas we would gather, and one person at a time would open a gift. As much as I appreciated what I had been given, I enjoyed even more seeing the joy on the faces of those receiving my gifts. The point is this: I believe a good way to honor your values is through philanthropy. You don't need to write big checks or wait for black-tie events to do good in the world. You can make a difference with what you own now: your time and your experience.

Open Horizons for Others

First, I should explain that Robby and I share a philanthropic philosophy that tends to be primarily focused on women, although not entirely. It wasn't so much a conscious decision as it was a result of the struggles I've faced as a woman in my industry, my efforts to help women succeed there, and the abuse I heard from my female clients.

Robby and I have a compound named *Broken Wing*, situated in a small town in Texas, where we host troubled individuals. We have invited high-powered women who have become so detached from life that they want to hurt themselves. We have brought in women who have had to fight so hard for their careers, and their piece of the pie, that they have had to sacrifice their own values. And we have hosted teenagers filled with anger and depression or consumed with peer pressure who need a respite from the bullying. Most are referred by clients or friends. After living in Los Angeles for twenty years, and through my many contacts in New York, I've found that many of our guests come from those two cities.

When they arrive, I welcome them onto the property and give them plenty of time to ride horses, walk through the gardens, cook with me, and do arts and crafts. I want everyone who comes to Broken Wing to reconnect with their inner child and to remember what they had forgotten along the way as they sought to claim the golden ring or achieve the American Dream. I encourage them to forget those voices whispering how they're never good enough and instead focus on small things: the wonder of nature, the smell of a horse in the morning, the digging up of garlic bulbs, the joy of puppies running to see you. Robby and I do our best to share what we have with our guests and give them whatever they need.

You can help people in the same way we do. You don't need to set up your own Broken Wing; you can invite troubled souls into your lives however it works for you. Help people in your neighborhood, your churches, and your personal clubs, or those you've heard about from friends. It doesn't matter who they are or what their problems might be; you can help them know that their problems don't need to be insurmountable obstacles. Your goal can be simply to help people in need interact with role models or experience a change of scenery. When you invite others into your lives, you open their horizons.

I'm an avid collector of South American, primarily Venezuelan, art. For years I traveled there to meet the artists and acquire their work. As it has become increasingly difficult to visit some of these countries, especially Venezuela, for safety reasons, I no longer choose to travel there. But that doesn't mean I've had to give up supporting the artists. In one case, an artist proposed a deal: He would gift me several of his most valuable paintings if I would give him a three-year stipend so he could escape to Paris to paint. There, he would be inspired and have access to more art supplies. (Yes, in Venezuela, artists even struggle just to get supplies.) I jumped at the opportunity, and Francisco Bellorin has gone on to become one of the great South American painters. He just recently passed away. Knowing that I was a small part in his development—and seeing some of his paintings in my own home—is more of a reward than I ever imagined.

Coming from Venezuela and witnessing the deterioration of my once incredible country, I also wanted to help immigrants making their way to the United States. The US provides the security and safety they yearn for, and it gives them the opportunity to make the lives of their children better. Wherever and whenever I can help, I'm available. I only ask for three things: learn our language, learn our culture, and abide by our laws. Then I encourage them to immerse and integrate their families into our country. I know that for many immigrants, leaving their country is not their first choice; it's a choice that's hoisted upon them under circumstances beyond their control. I was interviewed by Univision to tell the story of how Robby and I were helping these new immigrants adapt to life in America and to offer advice to others as to how they could do the same. You can view the interview here: www.univision .com/local/austin-kakw/si-trabajas-duro-todo-llega -asesora-en-riqueza-revela-las-oportunidades-que -todo-hispano-puede-obtener-en-eeuu-video.

I once received a letter from one of my new, young friends a few months after she arrived here from Venezuela at the age of six, along with her nine-year-old sister. The grammar and spelling are her own:

> Nora, thank you for everything that
> you have done for me. You teach me
> things that I never new that I will
> learn them or be good at it. You teach
> me how to belive in myself and I
> Never Give Up!

As they were leaving their country, the parents told the girls they would be going to Disney World in Florida; they had *not* told them they would not be going back home. The parents did this out of fear that the girls might say something to their friends and the authorities would find out. If that happened, the family would not have been allowed to leave the country—either their visas would have been denied or the family would have been intercepted at the airport. So the girls had packed accordingly and arrived in the US with only their small suitcases and the shirts on their backs.

The family had been friends of my half brother in Venezuela, so they knew to contact me as soon as they arrived. I immediately took these girls under my wing and provided the family assistance, which included finding them housing and helping them financially while the mother struggled with the language and the father tried to earn a living. Although the parents are both college-educated journalists, that didn't initially matter. As many immigrants have discovered after moving to America under these types of circumstances, they might have to restart life at the lowest rung. But even when immigrants are starting over, America offers them something much more important: opportunity and the freedom to re-create a safe and secure life.

This family has now been in the US for four years. The father eventually got a job with a major corporation. The entire family got their green cards and will soon be applying for citizenship. Like my brother Ivan and I did, the girls learned English quickly, and the oldest has graduated from high school and been accepted on an academic scholarship to a major Texas university. The mother is still struggling with English but getting better every day. To this day, I keep that little girl's letter hanging on my wall as a reminder of the joy I receive in giving back.

Control Where Your Money Goes

You might wonder why I help individual artists and families rather than sending money to nonprofits that are supposedly set up to help those in need, and you might consider my answer to that question heresy: Robby and I give in a way where we control how our philanthropic dollars are spent because most nonprofits seem to be very poorly run endeavors. I say that because I've discovered that most of the money they collect lands in the pockets of CPAs, attorneys, and friends and family in administration. Of course, some nonprofits run leanly and efficiently. But study after study shows how ineffective so many nonprofits are and what a small percentage of donations actually goes to help the causes they supposedly support.

The reason Robby and I give back is because it makes us feel wonderful, and we do it anonymously whenever possible. We currently pay for housing and care for several local individuals and families. This way we know exactly how our supportive dollars are spent. We also give to local animal shelters when they run tight on food or other needs; I simply go online to Amazon, purchase what is needed, and see that it's delivered. The animal shelters don't need to know where it came from. Robby and I know, and that's good enough. We have also helped numerous children who have amazing talent, but a lack of financial resources and/or parental guidance, by paying for some of their college costs or advanced training. I give away an endless number of books in an attempt to ignite minds. I take people, especially young girls, to exciting events they would never have otherwise been exposed to: a fancy dinner, an ice-skating exhibition, a sports game, or even just a manicure. I do this because I believe once people have discovered these experiences, their desire to repeat them will be motivating. And I don't need other organizations to spend my money to make this happen. I enjoy doing it myself.

Every summer I organize a camp for young girls between the ages of eleven and fourteen who don't have exposure to positive role models. I do it because I love outdoor activities, never had the opportunity to go to camp myself, and am constantly wanting to show young women the abundance of opportunities and experiences. While the focus is primarily on having fun, I also use the camp experience to show young girls what paths might be available to them—paths that most of them have probably never experienced or even knew existed. We dress up and go to an art museum. We have a spa afternoon. We hunt for archeological relics. We bring in instructors to teach the girls how to swim, how to kayak, and how to survive using their own strengths. They learn patience and logic by building with LEGO and engaging in various arts and crafts activities. They discover gardening, wildlife, golf, and Ping-Pong. They learn how to apply makeup and take care of their skin. And I make sure they learn about creating budgets and setting goals—something that is very lacking with all the young people I meet. Shouldn't "money" be taught in schools?

I'm not necessarily proposing that you do as I do by helping foreign artists, immigrants, animal shelters, or at-risk girls—although I can assure you, doing it the way I do makes it as rewarding for me as it is for them. What I'm saying is that you need to find something that makes you feel good about yourself by helping make the world a better place for others. It could be as simple as doing one daily good deed anonymously for someone you don't know. Or if you're going fishing, take along a boy without a father or a girl whose parents are going through a divorce. If you have an interesting job, invite a young adult from your place of worship to shadow you at work so you can show them your world. If you are an artist, visit with young budding artists at your local school, introduce them to your creations, and share your stories about struggle and success. Children and young adults will often be quiet and intimidated when invited to walk into someone else's life, so be gentle and patient. All you need to do is plant the seeds; you will reap rewards beyond your wildest expectations when you see them succeed later in their lives.

I have amazing friends who have taken this concept a step further. Well, maybe more than just one step: While on their way from Las Vegas to Florida, a couple with whom we have been longtime friends stopped in New Orleans to help with Hurricane Katrina's victims—and they never left. They decided to devote their lives to the Lower Ninth Ward, building homes for those who were displaced and taking in children who did not have parental guidance.

Another friend, after an eco-tour we took together, decided to devote her studies and life to indigenous Indians in Venezuela. Yet another friend quit her small, lucrative veterinary practice to establish spay/neuter clinics in underdeveloped countries. As you know, Robby and I made the conscious decision to not have children, so you could say this is our substitute: we help support all their efforts. I admire their passions. How awesome it is that they devote their lives to that which makes them happiest, and how awesome that we can be a part of it.

There are so many ways you can give back with your voice, your wisdom, or whatever you have to give. And there are so many people who not only need what you have to give, they deserve it. My wall is a testament to that; it's where I have posted numerous letters from children I've helped over the years. Let me close with another excerpt. This was from another girl:

"Nora, you have made such an amazing impact in my life. You have made me a better person in every way possible, and I can't thank you enough. You deserve the world and much more. Thank you for everything!"

CHAPTER TEN

PLAN FOR RETIREMENT—NOW

What would you do if you weren't afraid?

—Sheryl Sandberg, *Lean In: Women,*
Work, and the Will to Lead

T hough you may not be ready for retirement—or may not even have thought about it yet—retirement is a critical component of your life plan. Since it's an important component of my business, I started planning for my own retirement following one of my first classes in retirement certification at the age of twenty-two.

Plan Your Money

Planning out the income you'll need in retirement is one component of planning, and the second is planning out your time. Let's start with the money side since it's the most critical. I have consciously stayed away from quoting a bunch of statistics in this book, even though it would have been easy, given the business I'm in. I'm going to make an exception here, especially for my younger readers. The following statistics are important to know if you want to lead the life of your dreams in retirement, so take note.

It is often written that the upcoming generation does *not* want to work past fifty but *does* want to live to a triple-digit age. When planning how much money is needed for retirement, the "Multiply by Twenty-Five Rule" is commonly applied. This simplistic rule multiplies the desired amount of money you want to be able to draw from your retirement account annually, after you retire, by the number twenty-five. For example, if you want to withdraw $50,000 per year for twenty-five years, you'll need to have $1,250,000 ($50,000 x 25 = $1.25 million) in your investment portfolio when you retire. You can also look at it as the "4 Percent Rule" to arrive at the same conclusion. That is, a conservative rule of thumb is that once you retire, you can draw 4 percent annually from your portfolio if you want it to safely last 25+ years (4 percent x $1.25 million = $50,000).

What these rules don't account for is how inflation affects these needs based upon how long it is until you retire. The recent history of the buying power of the dollar indicates that, if you are twenty years away from retirement, you need to multiply your annual retirement income need by a factor of 2.19 ($50,000 x 2.19 = $109,500). What this tells you is that, if inflation continues at the same historical rate, you will need a retirement portfolio of $2,737,500 ($2,737,500 x 4 percent = $109,500) to have the same buying power twenty years from now that $50,000 gives you today. If you are twenty-five years away from retirement, you need to multiply by 2.67.

You can be assured that if you only want to work thirty years and retire at the age of fifty, reaching that goal, without a very nice inheritance, will not be an easy task. So if that is your plan, and an inheritance is not on the horizon, you need to get serious about saving and investing. Surveys show that two-thirds of working young adults have nothing saved, and only one-third participate in their employer's savings or retirement plan. Are you one of them?

Plan Your Time

Before I go further, let me point out that in Chapter 2, and in several other places along the way, I have talked extensively about planning and visualizing. Nowhere is applying the methods and advice on how to do those two things more important than in *planning for your time in retirement*. That said, let me change directions totally and tell you that, if you follow my next advice, you may not feel the need to fully retire quite as soon as you had been thinking.

In interviewing new clients, I ask three important and powerful questions about retirement. The first: "When do you plan to retire?" The second: "If you retired today, what would you do with your time?" And the third, after listening to their responses, whatever they might be: "Why not do it now?"

Let me first address questions one and two. Almost everyone has some type of trigger point on *when* to retire, such as at a certain age or when a pension vests. Personally, I love what I do and have integrated my career into my authentic life so well that I plan to continue what I'm doing as long as I'm physically and mentally up to the task.

It probably doesn't surprise you to hear that few of my clients have anything other a vague answer to *what* they will do when they retire. And almost none have made specific plans. When I hear this answer, I start the conversation by letting them know what I've observed. The first thing most people do is sleep in, with every day becoming like Saturdays used to be when they still worked. Their days go something like this: they get up, have a cup of coffee, eat breakfast, read, watch TV, and use their laptop. Then they start thinking about lunch and maybe do something around the house. Suddenly, it's afternoon. There will be an errand to run, and soon it's time to think about dinner. Newly retired clients often tell me how amazed they are that they ever had time to work! In retirement, the honey-do lists don't go away, and life's interruptions don't stop. You simply do not end up with endless hours to use for the hundreds of things you thought you might do, like learning another language, picking up snowboarding, golfing, or eco-traveling.

I also have clients who—like me—say they will never retire. My brother Ivan wants to practice medicine well into his eighties. Many type A executives do not want to retire because of the fear that they will *miss the action* or lose their mental capacities once they stop using them. In this situation, what I tell my clients, and myself, is that it's still important to be prepared to be forced to retire, usually due to the poor health of yourself or your spouse. This reality was recently brought home to me in the harshest possible way. A close relative in his mid-seventies, who owned his own business and, like me, had integrated it into his ideal lifestyle with no need or plan to retire, was diagnosed with late-stage cancer. Fortunately, he had done estate and succession planning—or the last months of his life would have been filled with stress and decision-making he was in no position to handle. Even for me, who has pretty much seen it all, this was an eye-opening personal experience and a brutal reminder to ensure my priorities have been set up for an unforeseen disaster. Being prepared for the unforeseen—and consciously addressing the "What will you do in retirement?" question—is critical to planning for retirement. Later in this chapter, I will cover specifically how I advise clients to be prepared for the unforeseen and the *what to do* part of retirement.

But now, let me address the all-important third question: "Why not do it *now*?" When I ask this, the most common response is a blank stare. I seldom get, and don't really expect, a good answer. When I do get a response, it's more in the form of rationalizations about *why not*, most of which are nothing more than excuses.

Depending upon the responses I hear, my advice then goes something like this: "You want to write? Go on a writer's retreat—now! You want to bottle your own beer? Do it in your garage—now! You want to be a volunteer firefighter? Do it on the weekends—now! You want to travel? Let's budget and plan for it—now!" I can assure you: international travel is best done in your younger years when you can still walk on cobblestones, don't have to worry about bringing along your required medications, and your back can handle a long overseas flight.

When I tell this to clients, they inevitably have a response as to why they are not already doing what they love. While that response may mention time or money, my experience tells me what they really need is someone to give them permission to do something other than work. That's where I come in. I'm the *do it now* person in their lives. I believe one of my most important responsibilities to my clients is not only giving them that permission, by assuring them they have the money, but also actively encouraging them to pursue these activities. And to do it *now*! The fact is, there *is* time in your working life to carve out and pursue these important activities and life goals. How do I know? I do it myself and have helped many of my clients do it as well. Remember how I helped Lauren visit the pandas in China? That was certainly something she neither wanted to wait to do until she retired, nor did she need to, and the experience changed the rest of her life. I can tell you from a lifetime of working with clients of all ages that the enthusiasm of youth does not grow as you age.

Watch for Detours and Obstacles

I also know from personal experience that waning enthusiasm is not the only obstacle we face as we age and retire. I have always loved to swim, but getting a breast cancer diagnosis in my forties put an end to that activity. It took me several years to go through a double mastectomy and reconstruction surgeries. And when I was finally cleared to swim, I tore my rotator cuff. Out again for another year! I'm finally able to swim again. Now, in my fifties, I swim every chance I get, and I feel great. If there comes a time when I can't walk, I will have Robby fix up a hoist to swing me into the pool so I can bob and soak to my heart's content.

I have seen clients make so many mistakes in anticipation of retirement. One of the most common is buying property for retirement. The reason why it's a bad idea is because it's a fact of life that, when you reach retirement, your dreams will likely have changed. That cute cabin in the mountains is too small. That coastal property in Oregon isn't really all that great. Maybe you'll find you no longer have the desire or health to build a home on that Canadian lake lot you bought while on an idyllic summer vacation there. What will happen if you and your spouse divorce or one of you becomes ill—or dies? Or if you decide you want to live closer to the grandchildren? While your plan may have seemed perfect in your younger years, it very likely will not seem so perfect when you retire.

I liken this to the battles I take on with several of my clients regarding buying time-share properties at any time in their lives. I have one client couple who *loves* time-shares. No matter how often or how strongly I advise against it, it seems as if they return from every trip owning another time-share. "The salesman was so nice, the property so beautiful, and the deal he gave us was so great that we just knew we'd want to return for a week or two every year, and we just couldn't pass up what we were assured was the opportunity of a lifetime." I'm sure it was, for the salesman at least. All you need to know is that after a year or two, I'm left with getting them out of a so-called investment property that they no longer want to visit or own. I'm sure you've heard all those "get out of your time-share" ads; I've got the experience to be an expert in that industry.

Use Caution with Sudden Wealth

Another situation, with challenges similar to retirement, is when clients suddenly come into a substantial sum of money, often an inheritance. Far too many make the mistake of immediately buying everything on their wish list. I have clients who have invested in multiple homes and then spent their time going from one home that has a mile-long list of to-dos to another one with another mile-long list. I had a client in his sixties with back problems who, upon receiving a sizable inheritance from his father, bought a Corvette—only to realize he couldn't get out of the low-slung seat. He had to return it, at a loss. I have had clients buy boats, but they had no time to enjoy them, and all the while their financial capital remained tied up in these water toys. I even had one client who bought a plane with his newly acquired wealth and then spent every dime trying to pay for the gas, the hangar, etc.

I understand how it goes: you fall in love with Italy while on a Mediterranean cruise and are tempted to buy the falling-down castle that you're just positive you'll fix up someday. Don't do it! Rent a villa for a few weeks. Likewise, rent a sailboat, or stay at first-class hotels, or rent luxury cars for the weekend, rather than buying retirement houses and other toys. Any option is better than buying. Once you retire, it's especially important that you manage, budget, and properly allocate resources to your dreams—but not go broke chasing them.

Take It Slowly

Whatever plans we've worked together to create for my clients' retirement, I advise them to take it slowly. Don't take on any jobs or new outside responsibilities for the first six months. That includes joining new boards, becoming more active in their places of worship, or participating in homeowner's association activities. The reason for this is simply to give yourself time to adjust. There is nothing wrong with getting a little bored. In fact, I contend that boredom is earned!

Once you retire, it's important to observe yourself to know what your body can do. Spend time adjusting to a new life with your spouse, family, and friends. If you find your needs and desires have changed after retirement, address them head-on. I can tell you from experience, and I've seen it way too often, that retirement can be a major problem for couples, especially for women whose career had been focused on the home and family. If this has been your situation, then over the years, your focus has been on raising your children, getting them through school, and then sending them off into their own lives. You have dealt with being an empty nester, and while your husband continued to pursue his career, you created a life for yourself that centered around your hobbies and friends. Now, suddenly, your husband retires. He doesn't know what to do with himself and looks to you to be his constant companion and playmate. Or worse, he doesn't want to go anywhere or do anything and expects you to wait on him. These are often the women who become my clients after their divorce.

Precisely for this reason, I ensure that all my clients' retirement issues are addressed long before retirement arrives. I have a plan discussed and drafted out, and it's updated regularly. And that plan does not start with a focus on money. It focuses on how the two of you—together—want to spend your retirement years. Money, of course, is an important part of planning and a major factor in deciding what you will be able to do. It is especially critical when there are elderly parents and still-dependent children to consider. The point is, unless they make a conscious decision to spend their retirement years separated—and I have had couples decide this—I often suggest couples counseling, specifically to address retirement issues, in order to prevent a crisis and avert the possibility of spending their retirement years in misery.

The important thing to remember is that retirement can be a truly wonderful time of life, provided, of course, that you have worked with your advisors and created a plan to enjoy it to the fullest.

CHAPTER ELEVEN

A LOOK INTO MY LIFE

The question of what you want to own is actually the question of how you want to live your life.

—Marie Kondo

You may have thought retirement would be the last chapter of this book, but I thought it would be more interesting and helpful if I closed by giving you a brief look into a day of my life. Some of what you are about to read I have touched on before; some will be new.

It has been said that behind every successful leader, professional, or CEO is the monotony of a habitual day. Leaders and doers intentionally organize and control their days to be repetitive. When I get out of my routine, I feel unmoored from life. While that is a feeling I love, I only want it when I'm on vacation and unplugged from work. It's not a feeling I want to experience midweek. Even when I'm traveling and waiting at an airport, or spending the night at a hotel, it's essential to my well-being and mental stability that I keep to my routine.

Getting the Day Started

For me, it's critically important to start each day being up-to-date on the political and economic complex in which I'm handling my clients' money. The US stock market is open from nine thirty in the morning to four in the afternoon EST, so my day is highly focused between those hours. Back in the day, I began each morning by reading numerous newspapers and then listening to the radio or television for updates on world matters. These days, I glance at my iPad first thing in the morning to look at premarket trading patterns and discover whether there have been any new calamities or changes in political/policy headwinds or any government movements around the world. I can also check in on war hot spots, the currency and interest rate markets, and corporate announcements. In my business, I cannot afford to sleep in, leisurely waking at ten in the morning and then figuring out what's going on. Too much will have already happened.

Once I have reviewed the world's affairs, I transition to my data bank of computers to do a quick review of my own activities, looking at what I did yesterday and refining my plans for today. Whatever your job, you need to do the same. You need to take stock of what you have accomplished and what is yet to be done. It does not matter if you do this in the morning or at the end of the day; that's up to you. Just make sure it's part of your daily schedule and that you do it the same way *every* day.

After I have completed this review, I decide what can be delegated and what I need to follow up on myself. This exercise helps bring me up to speed on where my team stands with projects, and it enables me to determine if and when new projects can or need to be started. By being organized, I'm prepared to handle the triage of life throughout the rest of the day, when clients call to report dire emergencies: a death in the family, an offer on their business, the birth of a new grandchild, a divorce in the works, a real estate offer accepted, and on and on. When the first round of issues has been addressed, usually by late morning, I like to call my other clients to discuss important matters related to them. I work on projects, analyses, and deadlines in the early afternoon, and only when absolutely necessary, I schedule appointments as well. As you will read in the next section, I reserve late afternoons for my *personal time*.

This daily routine is critical for me every day, but especially on Monday, which is often my busiest day. Everyone—clients, staff, family, and friends—tends to take inventory on the weekends and contact me on Monday with their updates and questions. By being organized and having a routine, I'm prepared to handle it all: prioritize those that need my help first, and then organize the others for when, and by whom, they will be handled. It's not just that this very organized routine helps with the normal events of the day; it's also critically important in allowing me to deal with the curveballs thrown my way. I recently mentioned a relative who was diagnosed with late-stage cancer. The call informing me of that came from my mother-in-law late on a Monday morning. If it were not for my organized daily routine, it would have been much more chaotic and difficult to find a way to free up the rest of my day so I could be available to help in any way possible. To me, nothing is more important than family.

Listening to My Needs

I want to stress the importance of learning about, and listening to, your body's own biorhythm. You have heard that some people are night owls and others are early birds. To truly know yourself, you need to know when you are most creative, when you do your best thinking, and when you are most effective at focusing on the tasks at hand.

While some people like to start the day with a run or doing laps at the gym, I have my meditation and swim time scheduled in the afternoon. I schedule it then for two reasons. The first is that it's after the market closes and therefore a time when I'm under the least stress and time commitments. The second is because I've learned, from observing myself, that it's the time of day when I am most creative and able to figure out solutions to problems or consider what I want to accomplish and how I'm going to get it done. As part of the process of reducing the stress of the day and getting my creative forces flowing, the afternoons are also when I play with my animals, work on arts and crafts projects, and spend time in the kitchen, cooking interesting recipes. And it's a critical time when I allow myself to just experience the daily joys of life.

By evening I'm mentally tired and need to rest and regroup. I am careful, if at all possible, not to schedule important business meetings in the evening because I know I'm not at my mental best. On evenings when I have no commitments, I go to bed around six, but not to sleep. This is my time to read—and nothing related to business! I like to read at least three books a month, including classic literature, contemporary novels, and how-to manuals. For me, reading is a tremendous tool to both learn and to escape. Haven't you always wanted to read a classic like Charlotte Brontë's *Jane Eyre*, a contemporary like any of Lee Child's Jack Reacher novels, or a how-to manual by an Arkansas farmer about raising chickens? I've read them all—and I did it last month! Today, many people like to listen to audiobooks or podcasts, but I like to read on my Kindle or the old-fashioned way: turning pages one by one.

Setting Goals

On a larger scale, Robby and I start each year making a list of what we want to accomplish, including the places we want to travel and the home and personal projects we want to tackle. I cannot say these personal activities take precedence over my work schedule, but they are treated as equally important, and they're consciously planned and scheduled. I have found this to be key to organizing and controlling my time and my life; otherwise, if I waited until I found available time for my personal projects, they would rarely get done.

For example, this year we decided to install a pool at our Texas home. We also decided to upgrade the boat dock at our home in Florida so we can easily, and in an organized fashion, have the time to fish when we are there. While I was actively involved in the planning stages, Robby was hands-on to oversee these projects. I'm happy to report both are near completion. A personal goal for me this year was to write this book. As I do with all things, I established a schedule. My schedule for writing was to take away from my reading time on Tuesdays and Thursdays, plus Saturday and Sunday mornings. As I neared the end, I devoted an entire week of what would normally have been vacation time to pull it all together. I also kept a notepad handy to jot down thoughts that seemed to come at all times of the day and night, as I assume most writers do.

At the beginning of each year, I set monthly and yearly business goals for myself. This year I hired Elisabeth, whom I consider an invaluable business partner, and I expect that she will one day take over my business. Along with that, I also expanded our support team. This allowed me to exponentially delegate more, thus freeing up my personal time to take on more clients and new projects. I also now have more time to ask and work on what I consider the fun questions regarding the business: How do we want to advertise? What committees do I want to devote more time to? What additional services can I offer my clients?

And at the end of each year, I make a commitment to myself to look back and assess. I grant myself permission to feel fulfilled with what I've accomplished and to find tremendous joy in celebrating the newness of what I have created—and especially how I've expanded my comfort zone. Everyone has a comfort zone, and it's my never-ending drive to expand mine. The longer you stay out of your comfort zone, the more expanded it will become and the richer your life will feel.

As an example, it was a huge step out of my comfort zone to hire Elisabeth. As you have probably assumed from all my tales of dealing with men in my industry, I have never felt comfortable trusting my business to anyone but myself—man or woman. Now that Elisabeth and I have worked together for almost an entire year, I know it could not have been a better decision. I now have someone (other than Robby, of course) to not only help deal with the day-to-day issues and problems, but also to share in the joys and accomplishments. And, as I had hoped and planned, we have been able to add a significant number of new clients.

In the course of writing this book, I relived many of the painful times I endured as a woman working in an industry dominated by men. As I did so, I repeatedly asked myself, "Why do I put up with all of this?" Today I know the answer: I love my clients. I have clients around the world, and I love that they let me into their lives, and I love being beside them on their life journeys. You may have thought my job was merely to manage other people's money, and yes, that is part of what I do. But it's so much more. My greatest joy is to give others permission to do what they really want. You want to move from Los Angeles to Kentucky and raise horses? I will help you get there. You want to take a sabbatical and explore Africa? I will help you organize that. You want to start an animal shelter in New Mexico? You want to become a Zen master? I will direct you to that path. I make no judgments about your desire. I will, however, tell you realistically whether you can do it and what it will entail to accomplish it. The rest is up to you.

Let me end this book by saying this: I'm told that less than 10 percent of the people who start reading a book such as mine—which offers insight and advice—read it to the end. For those of you who have, *thank you* for reaching this final page! I hope you have found a gem or two of wisdom along the way that will make your life more fun and, of course, wealthier. And never forget what it took me years to learn and what I've tried to convey here: *let nothing stand in your way*!

ACKNOWLEDGMENTS

I want to thank Robby, who has had to set his life aside during the hours it has taken me to write and publish this book. Robby, I want you to know how much I appreciate all you do to make our life wonderful, and I love you with all my heart. I also want to thank Robby's mother, Melinda—a realtor and also a trailblazer, a best friend, and the woman who taught me the importance of surrounding myself with beautiful things. And her husband, Doug, for his encouragement in writing this book and his assistance in organizing and editing it. I could not have had my voice heard without you.

Additionally, I want to express my gratitude to my business partner, Elisabeth, for her unwavering support and courage in embarking on this journey with me. I also greatly appreciate my dauntless personal and professional assistants, without whom I would not have had the bandwidth to complete this book.

I also want to thank Joanne Frasene for introducing me to the fabulous team at Girl Friday Productions—a team whose guidance and expertise made this project come alive.

And last but certainly not least, I want to thank all my clients, whose life stories have been woven into mine.

ABOUT THE AUTHOR

Nora Castro, a financial advisor and managing director at a financial advisory practice in Austin, Texas, has been the recipient of *Forbes*'s Top Women Wealth Advisors award every year since the award's inception in 2018. Castro received a bachelor of science degree in business administration from the University of Southern California and entered the financial services world at eighteen, joining a work-study program during college at a financial services firm. It was there Castro discovered a love for the industry and became that firm's youngest registered representative. Throughout her career, as a woman in a male-dominated industry, she has been ignored and belittled, yet she found a way to overcome the hurdles and open the barred doors she encountered along the way. As she will tell you, "The battles I fought and indignities I endured have left deep and everlasting scars. Hopefully, this book will make other women's career journeys less challenging."

Her career has been profiled in *Forbes*, and she speaks regularly at industry events for women's empowerment and at various charities, such as Texas Women for the Arts. *Open Your Own Doors* is her first book. She lives in Austin, Texas, with her husband, Robby.

NOTES

NOTES

NOTES

CPSIA information can be obtained
at www.ICGtesting.com
Printed in the USA
LVHW082124270921
698867LV00003B/5/J